The Bollywood Pocketbook of Iconic Characters

Diptakirti Chaudhuri is a marketer by day and a writer by night. He is passionate about and writes on Hindi cinema. He has written six books including three on Bollywood trivia, one on the history of Bollywood and one on legendary screenwriters Salim–Javed. He divides his time between his family in Bangalore and his work in Pune. Outside of real life, he can be found at his blog (diptakirti.com) and on Twitter (@diptakirti).

The Bollywood Pocketbook of Iconic Characters

Diptakirti Chaudhuri

First published in 2022 by Hachette India
(Registered name: Hachette Book Publishing India Pvt. Ltd)
An Hachette UK company
www.hachetteindia.com

1

ISBN 978-93-91028-39-8

Hachette Book Publishing India Pvt. Ltd
4th & 5th Floors, Corporate Centre,
Plot No. 94, Sector 44, Gurugram – 122003, India

Typeset in Arno Pro 11/16
Typeset by InoSoft Systems, Noida

Printed and bound in India by
Manipal Technologies Limited, Manipal

To Ma

'Humein tumse pyar kitna yeh hum nahin jaante,
magar jee nahin sakte tumhare bina…'

– From Chetan Anand's *Kudrat*
(written by Majrooh Sultanpuri)

Contents

Fearless Nadia

Hunterwali, 1935

'I am no devi!' Mary Ann Evans saucily told off Jamshed Wadia (of Wadia Movietone). The studio owner wanted to christen her Nanda Devi before launching her in movies, but she overruled him and carried on with her stage name – Nadia. It stood out at a time when Jewish or Christian actresses accepted Hindu screen names. But her screen name wasn't the only thing that made her stand out. She could swim, dance, ride horses and do gymnastics (including splits!) – pretty much everything an Indian stuntman could do at that time. Except speaking Hindi!

Following a career in ballet and a circus, Nadia tried her luck in films. After a few minor roles, the Wadia Brothers decided to gamble big on her with a genre-creating film, *Hunterwali*. The lead actress of the film was nothing like Indian cinema had seen before ... and since. Skimpy shorts. Knee-high boots. Sleeveless blouses. A cape. A Russian fur cap. A Zorro-like eye mask. And her signature whip.

On the first day of shooting, Nadia fought a bunch of villains on a rooftop and then executed a perfect jump from a great height. And then, she threw back her head and laughed! This laugh became a signature motif in her films. So did the epithet that director Homi Wadia gave her at the end of the first day's shooting – 'Fearless'. Her stunts in the film were crazier than anything male action stars had even attempted. Jumping on to chandeliers, heaving men on her shoulders, running atop trains... The presence of a 'bone setter' doctor was soon required on the sets. *Hunterwali*'s stunts were so outrageous that theatre owners didn't think they would be acceptable to an Indian audience. But when she cracked her whip on-screen and declared, 'From this day forth, call me Hunterwali', audiences – especially in the cheap seats – went wild. And there was no looking back.

Hunterwali became the most successful film of the season. Fearless Nadia spawned an entire genre of action films like *Miss Frontier Mail, Diamond Queen, Lutaru Lalna, Jungle Princess, Stunt Queen, Himmatwali, Toofani Tirandaz, Lady Robin Hood* and even a sequel, *Hunterwali Ki Beti*. Nadia took on the evils of

Indian society in film after film. Her name in *Hurricane Hansa* was a wordplay on her caste – Harijan – in the film and how she rose against upper-caste oppression. *Muqabla* was one of the first films to depict twins getting separated at birth, with one of them growing up to be a daredevil and the other one remaining docile.

Merchandise. Crazed fans. Massive box-office success. Nadia had it all. One wonders how Indian audiences (at the height of the freedom struggle, no less) accepted an actress with 'piercing blue eyes framed by corn-blonde hair' as Indian. But they did… and Fearless Nadia remained a top star appearing in over 40 films over a decade and a half. She was later hailed as a feminist icon as well. About her pioneering turn as an action star, journalist B.K. Karanjia paid her the ultimate compliment in the 1970s: 'The roles Amitabh Bachchan plays [now] are subtler versions of the roles played by Nadia.'

Alexander

Sikandar, 1941

'Aap ke saath kaisa saluk kiya jaye?'
'Jaise ek badshah ko doosre badshah ke saath karna chahiye.'

Alexander had defeated the Indian king Porus at the Battle of Jhelum (Hydaspes in Greek). And this exchange – made famous by Amar Chitra Katha and other Indian retellings – was the high point. From an Indian perspective, this is the most memorable part of Alexander the Great's campaign to reach the 'ends of the world'. This dramatic exchange puts the Indian king almost at par with one of world's most famous conquerors. While the historic veracity of this exchange is in some doubt, Porus's bravery and Alexander's graciousness in India are not. Which is why he was the first and only foreign invader with that ultimate accolade: A film with a title role!

Sikandar's director, Sohrab Modi – who also played Porus in the feature – deserves credit for helming a film of such scale. It successfully projected a foreign invader as the hero who finally meets his match in India. Modi started off in theatre. So he understood the importance of drama and dialogues, and *Sikandar* sparkles with its dramatic confrontations. Apart from that, the massive war scenes are brilliant too. With low-angle camera positions, these battle scenes were shot to make it look as if the army and the elephants are charging straight into the audience, almost like a 3D experience.

Sikandar was a massive success, with the public lapping up both the histrionics and the action scenes. Beyond the box office, it also captured the public imagination by showcasing an Indian king against a foreign invader. The colonial government banned it in army cantonment areas because of its patriotic undertones. Sikandar's success came from merging real history with some rousing elements of fiction. For example, in the movie, Alexander's Persian wife, Rukhsana, reaches India to tie a rakhi on Porus's wrist to ensure his safety. The film showed Alexander's army win thanks to its superior strategy. But their stealth attack under the cover of night ensured that the reputation of Indian soldiers remained intact.

Prithviraj Kapoor[1] as Alexander is a sight to behold. His strapping physique, light eyes and feline gait made him the perfect choice to play the Greek emperor. He was 35 years old at the time, almost the same age as Alexander himself. And his performance brought out the impatience and the insouciance of the upstart conqueror. *Sikandar* is one of Prithviraj's most memorable performances. He still hadn't acquired his gravitas. But it was a stepping stone towards the more regal roles he played later in his career that included Emperor Akbar in *Mughal-e-Azam*. And – in a reversal – King Porus to Dara Singh's Alexander in *Sikandar-e-Azam*.

---

1. Prithviraj Kapoor came out of the studio system for *Sikandar*. From being a salaried employee of a studio, he now became an independent performer commanding a (handsome) fee for every film. His earnings went a long way in funding his passion project, Prithvi Theatres.

Shekhar, the Anti-hero

Kismet, 1943

When *Sholay* ran for five years in Bombay's Minerva Cinema, it broke a 32-year-old record. This record was for a film which ran for nearly four years in a theatre – this time in Calcutta's Roxy Cinema. The film was *Kismet*, and it faced heavy criticism for glorifying a life of crime. The hero was a pickpocket and a conman, becoming Hindi cinema's first anti-hero.

Most of Ashok Kumar's earlier roles were that of a virtuous hero, improving societal conditions and doing good. This role was ground-breaking then. And he set the tone in the very first scene. When a jailer hopes that he won't have to see Ashok Kumar again as a convict, he cheekily replies, '*Meri toh hamesha yehi koshish rehti hai ki yahan na aaoo. Lekin kya karoon? Ek taraf main akela, aur doosri taraf* police *ka saara* department.' The character, Shekhar, is a thief, but is compassionate about the frail and the elderly. He can break into a millionaire's safe, but does so to raise money to help his girlfriend's family. With *Kismet*, Ashok Kumar created the template of the 'thief with a heart of gold'. This would go on to become extremely popular later, especially during the 1970s.

Ashok Kumar's earlier successes were mostly opposite Devika Rani. Since she was the bigger star, his own reputation as a bankable star wasn't fully made. *Kismet* changed that completely. His easy charm drew in a massive crowd, and *Kismet* became Indian cinema's first film to gross ₹1 crore at the box office. And Ashok Kumar himself became the first star of Hindi cinema, inspiring many other such anti-hero characters in noir-ish films. And that's not the only trend *Kismet* started.

A rich man's son leaves home after a fight. A thief then comes to steal from the rich man and drops his locket there by mistake. The rich man recognizes the locket as that of his long-lost son's. This lost-and-found formula using a family heirloom (and a tattoo) became a Hindi film staple. And the most famous teller of these tales – Manmohan Desai – credited *Kismet* as the original source code for his films. (Mehboob Khan's *Taqdeer* – also released in 1943 – had a lost-and-found incident happening at the Kumbh Mela, the mothership of this cliché.)

Kismet was truly an anti-establishment film – and not just because of the anti-hero character. The song '*Door hato ae duniyawale, Hindustan humara hai*' raised the hackles of the British government of the day. It was initially passed by censors because they thought the song asked the Axis powers – Germany and Japan – to stay away from India. They realised their folly when the song started getting used in rallies for Independence. The government went after the lyricist of the song, Kavi Pradeep, who had to go underground to evade arrest on sedition charges. In the film, however, conman Shekhar happily enjoyed the song. A Hindi film hero can be a conman, but never a traitor.

Raju the Tramp

Awara, 1951

Writer K.A. Abbas had heard a story about an uncle of his who was a sessions court judge. The judge's own son was accused of a crime and was tried in his father's court. Abbas and his co-writer, V.P. Sathe, wrote a script using this as the backbone of their story and first took it to Mehboob Khan – the leading film-maker of the times. Khan toyed with the idea of Dilip Kumar playing the title role and took a long time to give them a firm answer. The writers then took the story to Raj Kapoor, a new and upcoming director at the time, who didn't wait for a second after the narration finished. 'This script is mine,' he said, handing over a token amount to stake claim of the character who would go on to define him.

Awara's Raju is brought up in poverty and grows up to be a criminal after his father (Prithviraj Kapoor), a judge, abandons his mother, suspecting her of infidelity. He falls in love with lawyer Rita (Nargis), but continues his life of crime despite her attempts to reform him. Finally, a crime lands him in his own father's courtroom, as the father and son contemplate their injustices towards one another.

Awara's theme of 'nature vs nurture' was to showcase the class differences prevalent in the newly independent India and Raj Kapoor's desire for a 'new social order' in his country. He said *Awara* is 'the greatest juvenile romantic story wrapped in the poverty that the post-Independence era had inherited... and celebrates the innocence of the Republic, newly born, learning to cope with the difficult world'. Raju the Tramp has a good heart, but is unsophisticated and is often unable to handle an educated, modern woman. Much has been written about Raj Kapoor's concept of 'caveman love', which meant nearly manhandling his girlfriend in one scene as an expression of his passion for her. At the same time, in *Awara*, the woman in his life is also his moral compass. Nargis plays a lawyer who fights for Raj in court and makes a case for reforming the *Awara*. She would reprise this role of a morally upright woman in several other films with Raj Kapoor.

The most obvious influence in creating the Tramp was Charlie Chaplin, of whom Raj Kapoor was a big fan. The tramp in *Awara* (and later *Shree 420*) often dressed, behaved and executed gags just like Chaplin's famous character, though his issues were essentially Indian. '*Phir bhi dil hai Hindustani*,' as he jauntily explained later. Kapoor was also influenced by Italian neo-realism directors like Vittorio De Sica and Roberto Rossellini, giving voice to the underdog and speaking for the downtrodden in poetic representations of class conflicts.

Raju the Tramp became not only Raj Kapoor's but Indian cinema's most enduring character for several decades. Beyond India, in Soviet Russia, Turkey, China and other parts of Asia and Africa, the affable Raju lived on through *Awara, Shree 420, Anari, Jagte Raho* and *Jis Desh Mein Ganga Behti Hai*. Sometimes he was a misunderstood criminal, sometimes an idealistic do-gooder, sometimes a smart alec gone rogue ... To paraphrase a political slogan: Raju was India and India, Raju.

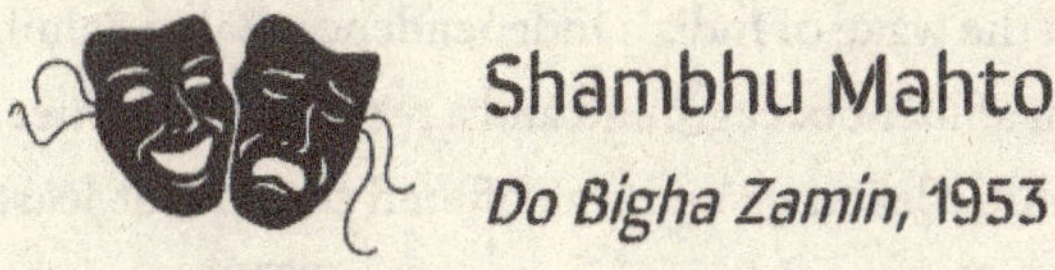

Shambhu Mahto

Do Bigha Zamin, 1953

For the first day of *Do Bigha Zamin*'s shoot, a nervous Balraj Sahni had prepped a lot to understand the nuances of the story and his character's motivation. As he stood ready for the day's first shot, director Bimal Roy gently told him, 'Wipe your feet before entering the zamindar's room.' With that one evocative detail, Roy breathed realism into Sahni's performance, which went on to get recognized as one of the greatest acting performances in Hindi cinema.

Do Bigha Zamin was based on a poem by Rabindranath Tagore, about a small farmer losing his land to a cruel zamindar. Bimal Roy, in his first film as a producer, also brought in the contemporary angles of urban migration and the debilitating poverty farmers spiral into due to usurious interest rates on loans. He was part of Indian People's Theatre Association (IPTA), and was influenced by the Leftist movement and was keen to portray social reality in the wake of India's Independence. Balraj Sahni, though from an affluent background and a recent UK returnee, also shared similar leanings and was offered the role at least partially because Roy saw his performances at IPTA.

In the movie, Shambhu Mahto, a farmer, is unable to repay a loan, and his land is attached by the zamindar. He moves to Calcutta and tries to earn enough money – by pulling a rickshaw – to pay back his loan and get his land released. Many misfortunes befall him, and he eventually returns to his village to see industrialization has reached there as well, with factories replacing farmland.

Realism was a key requirement, because Roy was inspired by Italian director Vittorio De Sica's *Bicycle Thieves* and decided to make a film about urban poverty in a totally real setting. To play this character authentically, Balraj Sahni regularly visited a milkmen's colony in Bombay to study their language, gait and posture. He travelled to Calcutta in a third-class compartment and, once there, he went to the rickshaw-pullers' union office and learnt how to pull a rickshaw, getting blisters on his feet as a result. During this stint, he met a middle-aged rickshaw-puller to whom he told the film's story. Halfway in, the man exclaimed, 'This is my story, Babu, this is my story!' Sahni later attributed the genius of his performance to this rickshaw-puller, whose soul he claimed to have imbibed.

Do Bigha Zamin was celebrated world over, nominated for the top prize at Cannes Film Festival, and became extremely popular in China and erstwhile USSR. The film's song '*Dharti kahe pukar ke*' even had Chinese and Russian versions.

In India, it was seen as a new kind of socially aware and progressive cinema, which told the story of a newly independent nation. It also cemented Bimal Roy's reputation as a major director in the industry and established his production house. And finally, it put in place the cruel moneylender–desperate farmer trope of Hindi cinema, complete with thumb impressions on ominously worded loan documents that would wipe out a poor man's life. Bimal Roy and Balraj Sahni had created a classic, which went on to become a template.

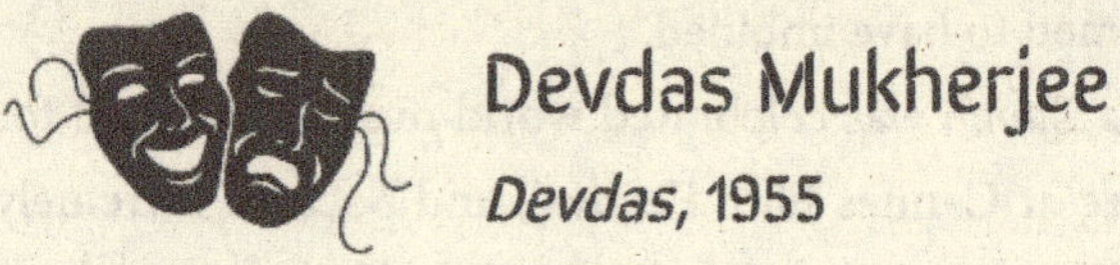

Devdas Mukherjee

Devdas, 1955

Feudal. Narcissistic. Coward. Degenerate. Purposeless. Prude. Sadomasochist. Alcoholic.

These are words selected from psychoanalytic studies[2] of India's favourite tragic hero. 'Virtually a generation wept over *Devdas*,' film scholars Erik Barnouw and S. Krishnaswamy wrote in their book, *Indian Film* in 1963. Two more generations have followed suit, and the love shows no sign of abatement.

Dilip Kumar was the quintessential *Devdas*. He had a talent for playing brooding and tragic figures, and was director Bimal

2. One of these studies is called *Devdas: India's Emasculated Hero, Sadomasochism and Colonialism* (by Poonam Arora). A rather unflattering description of Hindi cinema's most durable character!

Roy's first choice for the role. A succession of tragic roles had driven him into depression, and he had to take psychiatric help. One suggestion was for him to do more cheerful and swashbuckling roles, and he made a conscious attempt to do so in the 1960s. But *Devdas* remains one of his most iconic roles – remembered and referenced six decades after it released.

Dilip Kumar wasn't the first one to play Devdas though. Singer–actor K.L. Saigal first played the tragic hero in Hindi cinema in 1936 to great success, and the later version had huge expectations riding on it. Dilip Kumar – with his superior histrionics – performed the role with great finesse, making some of the dialogues quite legendary. '*Kaun kambakht hai jo bardaasht karne ke liye peeta hai? Main toh peeta hoon ke bas saans le sakoo…*' became the signature *Devdas* line, and was repeated by Shah Rukh Khan in Sanjay Leela Bhansali's much more opulent *Devdas* in 2002. It is amazing how the story of an alcoholic wallowing in self-pity still managed to find an audience in post-liberalization India. But the story had just begun.

In the last two decades, there have been more versions of *Devdas* than in the previous eight decades of the film industry. We even had a female Devdas, in a version (*Dev DD*) made for a streaming service. And somewhere along the way, the film versions of *Devdas* completely overshadowed the novel on which it was based. Bhansali's *Devdas* invented a dance sequence featuring the two heroines, though Paro and Chandramukhi never meet in the novel. (And indeed, how could they have? One was a rich zamindar's housewife. The other was a courtesan in a disreputable part of the city.) In Anurag Kashyap's *Dev.D*, contemporary events – an MMS scandal, a high-profile drunk-and-drive case – merged in the narrative, which ended happily, in a radical departure from the novel as well as the director's style.

'*Tu Devdas kyun ban gaya?*' is a standard taunt for moping lover boys. The phrase has come to symbolize a failed lover, drowning in alcohol and self-pity. The character was epitomized by Dilip Kumar and further embellished by others. In *Kaagaz Ke Phool*, Guru Dutt plays a director who gives a break to a newcomer (played by Waheeda Rehman). His film becomes a hit, the actress becomes a star and eventually leaves him. The director is broken, loses his money and status, eventually dies alone in a deserted studio. The movie he had made was *Devdas*.

Radha

Mother India, 1957

When Nargis and Sunil Dutt got married in March 1958, Mehboob Khan, the director of their latest blockbuster – *Mother India* – couldn't attend the wedding ceremony because he was in Los Angeles, preparing for the Oscar ceremony. *Mother India*, India's first submission to the Oscars, was one of the nominations for the Best Foreign Language Film. Mehboob had to excise the hammer and sickle from his company's logo to avoid being branded as Communist in USA. He also had to seek help from Prime Minister Jawaharlal Nehru to sanction foreign exchange that would allow him to send a subtitled print to the Academy to consider and for him to attend the ceremony. Quite fittingly Nargis also joined him, though Mehboob had a heart attack on the night of the awards ceremony (but he was able to recuperate quickly).

Mother India was a remake of Mehboob's earlier hit, *Aurat* – an evergreen theme, if there was one. A woman, Radha, has every conceivable misfortune unleashed on her. She stoically weathers every single one of them and brings up two sons. One is dutiful, while the other is a rebel, who leaves the village to become a bandit. When he returns to take revenge on the village moneylender – his mother's bête noire – the mother pulls out a gun on him for bringing dishonour to the village. '*Tu mujhe nahin maar sakti. Tu meri maa hai,*' the son taunts. '*Main ek aurat hoon... Main beta de sakti hoon, laaj nahin,*' she retorts dramatically before shooting down her son in a scene forever etched in the audience's memory.[3] The sacrifice of her son for the sake of her nation is a standard filmi mothers have been living up to for the last 60 years.

Mother India is a Nargis tour de force. She was in her mid-twenties when she took on the role, and the movie showed her age from a young bride to an elderly mother bringing up two

3. This tour de force was written by Wajahat Mirza, whose dialogues became templates for several films in the future. Mirza also wrote the dialogues for the legendary *Mughal-e-Azam* and *Gunga Jumna*, among others.

sons. It was also one of the last films she acted in, marking the end of her RK phase, when she dissociated herself from Raj Kapoor after their romance ended. She had refused to do *Phagun* with him because it required her to age on-screen, but had gone ahead with *Mother India.* She also met Sunil Dutt, her on-screen son in the movie, who heroically saved her from a ghastly fire on the sets and the couple fell in love almost immediately (and married soon after).

Mother India is one of the most influential films of Hindi cinema and, adjusted for inflation, is still one of the most successful. Beyond its commercial success, *Mother India* created enduring themes for several generations of Indian films. Two brothers on different ends of the moral scale and the loving but duty-bound mother would be used most notably in *Ganga Jumna* and *Deewaar,* which spawned further clones. (Ironically, a lavish sequel, *Son of India,* flopped at the box office.) No list of must-watch Hindi films is complete without *Mother India,* and Nargis carrying a plough in a Christ-like pose of suffering is an iconic image. She came to be identified with the role, her moral rectitude in the face of distressing poverty becoming a (somewhat idealistic) symbol of Indian motherhood.

Roop/Raja–Neeta

Dil Deke Dekho, 1959

A couple separates due to the machinations of a villain. The poor parent takes their son and moves away. The son grows up and takes up a job at the other (rich) parent's estate. He falls in love with a girl raised by the rich parent. Villain sends his son to pose as the rich parent's long-lost son and creates a misunderstanding with the real son. Of course, everything is sorted out eventually.

Nasir Hussain, the master of Hindi film entertainers and the king of formulas, used this exact recipe five times with only the cast changing (but not by much either). It started with his first directorial venture, *Tumsa Nahin Dekha,* where he also found his favourite star – Shammi Kapoor, who came out of the shadow of his elder brother and modelled himself as a 'Rebel Star' (with exuberant shades of Elvis Presley). It was the start of a very successful journey of playing the handsome, singing–dancing rake in a series of romantic comedies through the 1960s. With his second film, *Dil Deke Dekho*, Hussain found the female lead of many of his films, Asha Parekh. Both were cast in his own image. Nasir Hussain's biographer, Akshay Manwani, suggests that Shammi Kapoor's flamboyant, stylish persona was a reflection of the director's younger self. And Asha Parekh became something of a muse – as they were both in love with each other and she was part of every film of his till 1971.

Raja (Shammi Kapoor) of *Dil Deke Dekho* is a Western musician, a profession he made even more famous in *Teesri Manzil*. The music (by Usha Khanna) was frothy and foot-tapping, something of a 1960s trademark. Raja and Neeta (Asha Parekh) are not the usual lovebirds-at-first-sight couple, but they have a few fights before they fall in love – another Nasir Hussain hallmark. Comedian Rajendra Nath made his debut and was soon to become a common fixture in Hussain's films as well. And the story was – of course – an iteration of his earlier *Tumsa Nahin Dekha*, which would be further repeated in *Jab Pyar Kisise Hota Hai, Phir Wohi Dil Laya Hoon* and *Pyar Ka Mausam*.

This mix of estranged families, mistaken identities and romantic cat-and-mouse would become a staple of Hindi cinema of the 1960s. After the idealism and social messaging of the 1950s, the Hindi film audience wanted something lighter and more colourful. This template – started and perfected by Nasir Hussain – became what can be called 'hill station romances'. Shammi Kapoor, Joy Mukherjee, Biswajeet and the like acted in several of them, many of which became majorly successful and almost representative of the cinema of that time.

Nasir Hussain's son, Mansoor Khan, recalls making fun of his father's films. He felt there were too many coincidences happening, and the same story was used over and over again. The genial Nasir Hussain would accept this criticism good-naturedly, but ask, '*Lekin mazaa aaya ki nahin?*' Well, we all know the answer to that one!

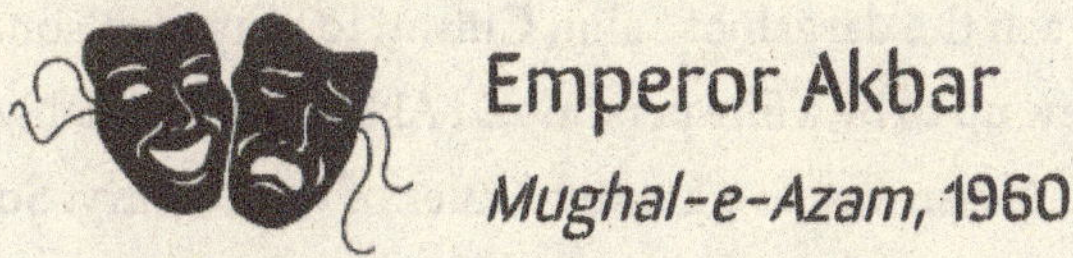

Emperor Akbar

Mughal-e-Azam, 1960

Mughal-e-Azam's cinematographer, R.D. Mathur, was astounded when he heard the price of the shoes. Akbar was supposed to wear them in the film and the director, K. Asif, had insisted that his production department get him shoes with real pearls embedded on them. The cost of the shoes was an astronomical Rs 3,000 (remember, this is in the late 1950s). Mathur wondered if the expense was justified, because there weren't any close-up shots of the shoes in the movie. K. Asif replied, 'When my Akbar wears those shoes and walks, he will feel every inch an emperor and that expression is what the camera will capture.'

Mughal-e-Azam was the first grand portrayal of Akbar the Great, and it embellished – even introduced – many stories about him. Akbar was a loving, doting father. He walked barefoot on hot sand to reach the dargah of Salim Chishti to pray for a son. A son who grew up to be a fine person and Akbar was justifiably proud of him. Akbar was also a dutiful ruler of the country. So when his son rose in rebellion for love, Akbar thought nothing of going to war against him. His unreasonableness in the face of his son's romance with Anarkali was somehow justified by his desire to maintain the world order. Akbar was also kind, and a fair dispenser of justice. He did everything in his power to end his son's affair, but compromised in private to save Anarkali's life – who actually hadn't committed any crime. Akbar was secular. When he was getting ready for war, a Brahmin priest and a mullah both said prayers for his victory.

The secular credentials of Akbar were further cemented by Ashutosh Gowariker's *Jodhaa Akbar,* the love story we never read about in textbooks but seemed perfectly plausible. Akbar's policy of Rajput alliances got a filmi makeover as Rajput valour and Mughal honour played a visually spectacular game of war and peace in the film. Akbar was a romantic, wooing his initially reluctant wife with flair and fervour. Akbar was brave, not averse to taking on the enemy king in a one-on-one battle to save the lives of their foot soldiers. And Akbar also had six-pack abs and rippling muscles, the kind that keep women awake at night!

Historians have analysed Akbar and his rule through facts and logic, and sometimes with a wee bit of ideological bias. The scriptwriters of Bollywood have portrayed the character with flourishes that can only be accorded by fiction, bound only by the thinnest strands of historical events. Thanks to the cultural insinuation of Hindi cinema, many of these stories became 'truths' for large parts of the populace. Emperor Akbar of Bollywood has turned out to be more charismatic, more just and (of course) more handsome than the real one we called Akbar the Great.

Vijay/Munna

Half Ticket, 1962

Kishore Kumar was in Madras to shoot a film called *Miss Mary*, but he wasn't called to the sets for five whole days. Bored and angry in his hotel room, he started chopping off his hair till there was virtually nothing left on his head. Another time, he arrived on set with make-up only on half his face because the producer had paid him just half his fees. Kishore Kumar held a dim view of most of his directors, and his eccentric run-ins with producers and directors were of legendary proportions. Producer–director Kalidas Batabyal – also brother of actor Pradeep Kumar – was so fed up with Kishore's antics that he reported him to the income tax authorities, leading to a raid (and a lifetime of altercations). Kishore got his revenge by inviting

Batabyal home and then locking him up in a cupboard for two hours. The film they were shooting was *Half Ticket*.

Loosely based on the Hollywood film *You're Never Too Young*, *Half Ticket* was the cinematic manifestation of Kishore Kumar's lifelong flirtation with sanity and lunacy. The film starts with Vijay (Kishore Kumar) having frequent run-ins with his industrialist dad for his socialist leanings. Everything about the film had a tinge of Kishore-induced lunacy, including Vijay's dead mother in a photo frame – which was Kishore Kumar in drag. The skeleton of the plot is about Vijay pretending to be 12-year-old Munna in order to travel on a half ticket. And the brilliant costume – a shirt, shorts with suspenders, a cap, a scarf and teddy bear – takes it to the next level. A second plot point is about a diamond smuggler (Pran) slipping a diamond into his pocket. The resultant chase has him changing costumes, making wisecracks and eventually singing a full song in drag – both male and female voices sung by him. The romance with Madhubala could have been conventional, but even that has a twist with Madhubala having to babysit Munna.

Film critic Sukanya Verma says, 'You can find *Half Ticket*'s echoes and reference in so many movies. Whether it's Amitabh Bachchan's Mausi-scene in *Sholay* or the way he goes about demolishing an entire conference in *Namak Halal* or Govinda's

Munna-inspired Sunder in *Jaan Se Pyaara* or "*Cheel cheeli*" dance in *Partner*, they all contain a trace of Kishore Kumar's antics from this 1962 comedy.' Given Kishore Kumar's predilection for this version of comedy and his aversion for the director, much of the panache and spontaneity he brought into the role was just by being himself. In an interview, Kishore Kumar said that after he shaved off his hair in Madras, '... they said I had gone cuckoo... [I] found everyone wishing me from a long distance and keeping a safe distance of ten feet while talking.' When you see the aghast expressions on the supporting cast in *Half Ticket*, you'll realize that Kishore Kumar was Munna and Munna was Kishore Kumar.

Kalyani

Bandini, 1963

After the success of *Sujata*, Nutan was obviously Bimal Roy's first choice for *Bandini*. But when he made her the offer, she was already married and didn't want to act in films any more. When she informed him of this decision, the normally reticent Bimal Roy simply said, '[Then] I won't be able to make this picture. I will have to look for another story.' Thankfully, Nutan relented, and the film got made.

Bandini, Bimal Roy's last directorial venture, perfectly showcased the dynamic combination of Bimal Roy and Nutan – their first partnership being *Sujata*. Roy was known for his sensitive portrayal of women. Most of his female protagonists were strong-willed, intelligent and memorable. *Bandini*'s Kalyani starts with being a courier for freedom fighters, refusing to be just a woman in the kitchen, whose only job is to feed revolutionaries. She falls in love with a freedom fighter (Ashok Kumar), not as a wallflower but as a partner of his dreams of independence. When he abandons her, she is strong enough to leave her village in order to spare her father the ignominy of her failed relationship. She takes up a nursing job, which she performs dutifully until she murders a patient when she reaches a breaking point. In prison, she is a devoted and efficient nurse with whom the prison doctor (Dharmendra) falls in love. He loves her enough to persuade his family to accept her – a murder convict – as their daughter-in-law. But, in the climax, she gives up that life of relative comfort and chooses to leave for an unknown destination with her first love, the freedom fighter, who is now terribly ill.

Bandini has one of the boldest acts by a heroine in Hindi cinema. Kalyani works as a caregiver to a neurotic harridan, who turns out to be the wife of the man she loves. She tries her best to do her duty despite the abuses heaped on her. Eventually, she cannot take it anymore and poisons the woman, going to jail for her crime. It is to the director and actress' credit that a Hindi film heroine came out of her perennial sacrificial lamb mode and did something so radical on-screen – that too in the 1960s. Even more creditable was the depiction of her hatred and anger slowly mounting, which looked natural and set the stage for the audience (and the hero) to forgive her.

Bandini was a quietly path-breaking film. And the soft-spoken Kalyani is one of the most remarkable female characters in Hindi cinema, who performed all her duties and lived by her own high moral standards. Director Sriram Raghavan watched the film several times while preparing for *Ek Hasina Thi*, a large part of which was set in a women's prison.

Bandini was a critical success and swept the awards season, taking prizes for both Best Director and Best Actress at Filmfare. More importantly, it established Nutan as one of the powerhouses of acting in Indian cinema. It was her third Filmfare award, and she went on to win two more to create a record (that's yet to be broken and, so far, has only been equalled by her niece, Kajol). Bimal Roy's reputation as a legendary director needed no further endorsement, but it was a worthy swansong, getting him his seventh and last award for Best Director.

Master Pillai

Padosan, 1968

A Bollywood legend goes that Mehmood was doing odd jobs in and around the film industry when he asked his good friend and established star, Kishore Kumar, for a role in one of his movies. Kishore Kumar is said to have famously responded, 'How can I give a chance to someone who will compete with me?' And Mehmood supposedly replied, 'One day, I will become a big film-maker and I will cast you in a role in my film!'

And indeed, when he produced a film for the first time, he cast Kishore Kumar in a pivotal role. And the film is still considered one of Hindi cinema's most durable comedies – *Padosan*.

Mehmood's dream of making a film with the industry's best comic talents culminated in this film, and he led the line-up himself as Master Pillai, the heroine's 'Carnatic' music teacher. In the 1960s, Mehmood had wrested away the 'best comedian' tag from Johnny Walker, and had acted in so many hit films with a rollicking comedy track that he was as big a draw as most heroes. He sold tickets and was a prominent part of posters. Hence, producing a movie, in which he played the lead, was a sound commercial decision.

Padosan's plot (based on a Bengali short story *Pasher Bari*) – a tuneless boy, Bhola (Sunil Dutt) trying to woo a music-loving girl (Saira Banu) with the help of his musically inclined friends, including Vidyapati (Kishore Kumar) – was the perfect vehicle to pack gags into. The verbal and physical comedy was bolstered by two other geniuses – R.D. Burman and Manna Dey. Dey provided the playback voice for Master Pillai,[4] whose vocal callisthenics matched Bhola and Vidyapati note for note, though he lost in the end (something the classically trained Dey was a little miffed about). Saira Banu recalled that the shooting

4. The musical showdown was a song '*Ek chatur naar*', which borrowed the opening lyrics from a similarly named song in a 1941 film called *Jhoola*. Composed by Saraswati Devi (who was incidentally a Parsi with a mouthful of a name, Khursheed Manchershah Minocher-Homji), the lyrics were written by Kavi Pradeep and the song was performed onscreen by Ashok Kumar (with a distinctly comic touch).

of the film was replete with retakes because the cast and crew could barely control their laughter during takes.

It is said that Mehmood not only produced but ghost-directed the film as well. *Padosan* – coming in quick succession after his hilarious roles in *Pyar Kiye Jaa* and *Gumnaam* – established him as a comic superstar for several years to come. Along with *Gumnaam*, *Padosan* also perpetuated a South Indian stereotype in Bollywood, which ended up becoming something of a caricature. Nevertheless, this observation cannot be made while watching the film, because the comedy is too hysterical to even take a break from laughing.

At the end of *Padosan*, all turns out well in a filmi sort of way. Bhola wins the girl, and Master Pillai is seen tearfully playing the shehnai at their wedding. An irony considering that Mehmood once said many heroes of the time refused to work with him: 'Not because I would steal the show, as everyone thought, but because I'd steal their girls!'

Idealistic Nation Builder

Satyakam and *Aadmi Aur Insaan*, 1969

'*Fhookh, bekari, black marketing sab khatam ho jayenge…*,' discuss two young engineers in the opening scene of *Satyakam*, as they graduate at the cusp of India's Independence. Of the two, Satyapriya (Dharmendra) is more than eager to face the world, filled with energy and idealism, believing his technical knowledge will lay the foundations of the newly formed nation.

'*Yeh [desh ki] mitti pyaasi hai. Jis din iski pyaas bujh jayegi, yeh mitti sona ban jayegi. Aur bahar ke deshon se bhik maangne ki zaroorat nahin padegi*,' says Munish (Dharmendra, again), while overseeing the construction of a dam after returning from abroad with an engineering degree, believing his foreign education will be of greater use in this developing country.

It is probably an indicator of the zeitgeist of the late-1960s that two directors as diverse as Hrishikesh Mukherjee and Yash Chopra selected stories about an idealistic engineer facing corruption and being branded a troublemaker. Mukherjee's Satyapriya refuses to compromise even one bit as he rejects bribes, bristles against nepotism, fights his superiors and refuses to even temporarily use official furniture for personal use. In his book on Hrishikesh Mukherjee, film writer Jai Arjun Singh likens Satyapriya to Yudhishthir. Satyapriya falls in love with a 'fallen woman', but is unable to express his feelings and marries her only to save her from the ignominy of rape. Chopra's Munish is flamboyant and fun-loving, but is almost as principled as his doppelganger. His refusal to adopt nefarious tactics at work leaves him without a job. He wavers towards the end, out of a sense of loyalty towards a friend who made his life (though his friend's conscience awakens in time).

Hrishikesh Mukherjee calls *Satyakam* his favourite film, though it is very different from the light-hearted films he is most known for today. It is also a difficult film to watch, with the principled hero going from one crisis to another – unable to bend his principles, causing harm to himself and his family. Farooq Shaikh once said, 'I can still not see *Satyakam* without it wrenching me and turning my stomach inside out.' Such unflinching commentary and the tragic end kept audiences away, and probably paved the way for the slew of lighter films Mukherjee directed in the 1970s and 1980s. Yash Chopra started his career with two films – *Dhool Ka Phool* and *Dharmputra* – that had strong social messages. While *Aadmi Aur Insaan* was in the popular mould of filmmaking, the idealism of its protagonist was a strong message against the institutional corruption seen to be spreading in India then. It did not do too well commercially either.

In both cases, the hero was a failure or only partially successful in his quest to reform the system – not an ending the audiences were satisfied with. This slowly-building national frustration manifested a few years later in the form of the 'Angry Young Man', while this idealistic nation builder remained a symbol of satyagraha in the centenary year of India's greatest *satyagrahi* – Mohandas Karamchand Gandhi.

Flight Lt Arun Verma

Aradhana, 1969

'Goodbye Flight Lieutenant Arun. I'll miss you. We all will,' Sharmila Tagore wrote in the *Hindustan Times* on 19 July 2012, echoing the nation's sentiment, the day after Hindi cinema's first superstar passed away. He played Flight Lt Arun Verma in *Aradhana*, the film that started a phenomenal streak of 17 consecutive superhits starring him. The definition of the term 'superhit' is hazy, and the streak of 17 becomes 15 as per some records. But what is indisputable is the hold Rajesh Khanna had over the country between 1969 and 1972.

Rajesh Khanna was chosen for *Aradhana* because he had won a contest organized by Filmfare and United Producers, a consortium of film-makers, which included Shakti Samanta, who directed and produced the film. And he was cheap, to be paid only Rs 35,000 as per the contract he signed when he won.

Strictly speaking, Rajesh Khanna's hit run started with Yash Chopra's songless thriller *Ittefaq*, in which the young actor played a murder accused on the run. It was as different from his romantic image as it could get, and *Aradhana* – released two weeks later – is the landmark film that kick-started the Rajesh Khanna juggernaut. From the moment he appeared in a jeep next to a toy train singing '*Mere sapnon ki rani kab aayegi tu*', Hindi film audiences couldn't get enough of him. And themes from *Aradhana* would be repeated many times in his later successes, making it the definitive Rajesh Khanna film.

And the Rajesh Khanna archetype was a hardworking, self-sufficient man let down by circumstances. In *Aradhana*, it was a war, while it was terminal diseases, bad marriages and societal oppositions in other films. The other constant was tragic, uplifting love. In his biggest hits, Rajesh Khanna's romance remained unrequited (due to a sacrifice) or faced stiff resistance before the culmination. *Aradhana*'s romance was cut short by a plane crash, before the son arrived and gave meaning to the characters' (and audiences') lives. And finally, there was music. Rajesh Khanna's career was made by the partnership of Kishore Kumar and Rahul Dev Burman. It is said that Sachin

Dev Burman (the official composer for *Aradhana*) was unwell during the making of the film, and it was his son who recorded the final soundtrack, even composing parts of it. Kishore Kumar, who was more of an actor in the 1960s, resurrected his singing career with *Aradhana*, and became the voice of Rajesh Khanna.

Aradhana also started a phase of women fans writing letters to the actor in blood, marrying his photos, kissing his car as it left studios and screaming his name outside premiere venues. It is for this crazed following that Rajesh Khanna is called Hindi cinema's first superstar – such a loyal fan base had never been seen before or since. In these days of millions-strong social media following, this might sound like an exaggeration. But let it be known that the person who has repeatedly corroborated Rajesh Khanna's unique status is one Amitabh Bachchan. And he knows a thing or two about stardom.

Monicaaaaaaaaaaaaaaa

Caravan, 1971

Helen was dancing in films since she was in her early teens, and she was not only the most popular dancer but also the most efficient. Having a Helen song in a film did a lot for its commercial prospects and she usually managed to shoot an entire song in a single eight-hour shift. Only once did a song take about 10 to 12 days to shoot. The song was '*Piya tu ab toh aaja*', often called her most iconic.

In Nasir Hussain's *Caravan,* Helen plays the role that she was often given when her character needed to do more than just dance. As Monica, she is the villain's long-term girlfriend, who plots with him to ensnare the heroine (Asha Parekh) into a marriage, so that she can be killed and her property usurped.

Helen plays the vamp with aplomb – first involved in double-crossing the heroine and then having a change of heart when she realizes her boyfriend isn't beyond killing her either. She starts trying to help the lead pair and provides them with vital clues to solve the heroine's father's murder. While this sounds like a spoiler, it isn't at all. This is the role she played best. And often.

In another Nasir Hussain production, *Teesri Manzil*, she played an equally memorable role. She is the dancer in the hotel, who drops cryptic hints to the hero and controls the flow of information from the background. Her role in *Caravan* was in the same mould, but her actions involved more brains – which she called 'fool-proof drama'. She manages to scare the just-married heroine into a brake-less car by revealing proof of her husband's shenanigans. And then she managed to put the husband in a tight spot using the same evidence. But Helen's histrionic turn in *Caravan* was lost to her legendary dance number, which started with an unseen admirer calling out her name: 'Monicaaaaaa, oh my darling!'

R.D. Burman's biographers Anirudha Bhattacharjee and Balaji Vittal say, '*Piya tu* became the quintessential Pancham–Asha duet... This song was like a scream against traditionalism.' And Helen plays the lustful woman unable to control her desire for the unseen lover. She pants, writhes, prances, dances and finally fixes herself to the man in a dance that's simultaneously an erotic performance and a love story. It is to Helen's eternal credit that she performed about 500 such numbers (as per unreliable estimates), and made them all look fresh and exciting. Helen had been performing for more than 20 years when she played Monica and continued for a decade more as Bollywood's premier seductress. She was – as the announcement before '*Piya tu*' went – '*Hindustan ki mashoor* cabaret dancer, *the one and the only one, Monica.*'

Janice

Haré Rama Haré Krishna, 1972

Dev Anand was shooting for *Johny Mera Naam* in Kathmandu when the hippie movement was spreading across the world, and he had his first brush with this group. These unkempt youngsters had taken over the city – easily noticeable due to their distinctive clothing, libertarian ways and, most visibly, their consumption of drugs. In the mostly white crowd, Anand came across an Indian–Canadian girl. After a few meetings, she told him her story. She had left her divorced parents, and was seeking enlightenment and peace in this commune. Her original name was Jasbir, though everyone called her Janice.

Dev Anand's script captures this story faithfully, but he couldn't find his heroine from the industry because (a) none of the older heroines would suit the mini-skirted, svelte character he had in mind, (b) a role which showed the heroine smoking and drinking wasn't something Bollywood heroines wanted to play, and (c) playing the hero's sister meant being typecast in 'sister' roles forever. The right actress turned out to be a rank newcomer; the winner of a beauty contest – Miss Asia.

Zeenat Aman was the daughter of screenwriter, Amanullah Khan, but having grown up with her German stepfather and having spent time out of India, she was completely unaware of Hindi cinema's norms. And she fit into Janice's role like a glove. Wearing oversized goggles, wide hairbands, printed dresses and with an Anglicized accent, her performance was spot on. As the misguided youngster who gets embroiled in drugs and shady company, she was easily the most noticeable character in the film. And her song, '*Dum maaro dum*' became a youth anthem.

Once *Haré Rama Haré Krishna* released, Aman became an absolute sensation. She became the new sex symbol, and a very different one at that. Her 'flower child' role broke all the pre-conceived notions about Bollywood heroines and created space for roles that were modern, sexy and uninhibited. All this while, the skimpy dresses, smoking and drinking were left to the vamps, while heroines remained chaste. If a heroine got involved in any of these transgressions, she usually died as penance!

Zeenat Aman was part of the new breed of heroines who could out-Helen Helen in their day. She was immediately signed on by Nasir Hussain for *Yaadon Ki Baaraat* and Dev Anand himself for *Heera Panna* (and *Ishk Ishk Ishk* after that).

In the next couple of years, Bollywood saw the debut of two stars in a similar mould. Dimple Kapadia debuted as *Bobby* – another modern-day teenager, in bikinis and 'with it' outfits. Parveen Babi, a model, transitioned to films, and soon hit the big time with her pairing with rising superstar Amitabh Bachchan. Both Zeenat and Parveen fit in Bachchan's films, many of which were about anti-heroes, and the heroines were not expected to be docile, homebound *sati savitris*. Their figures, their fashion sense and their style ensured that Bollywood now had a new kind of heroines.

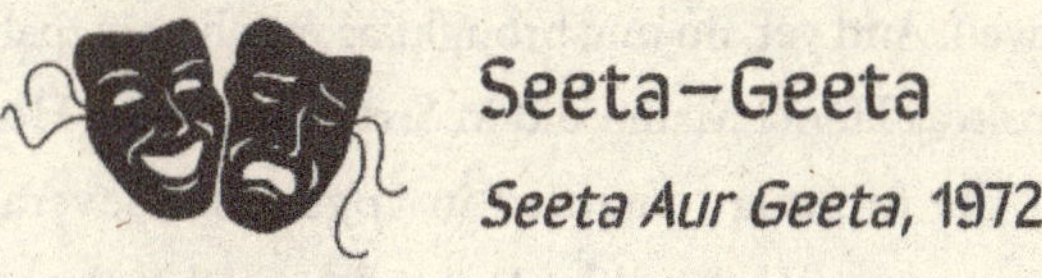

Seeta–Geeta

Seeta Aur Geeta, 1972

The first scene Hema Malini shot for *Seeta Aur Geeta* was in a police station. Tomboy Geeta has been brought in, but docile Seeta's family is called to hand her over. In a crazy comic scene, Geeta has to climb atop a ceiling fan. To assure her of the fan's sturdiness, director Ramesh Sippy got a ladder, climbed and sat on the fan himself and swung around for a bit. Hema Malini followed suit and transformed into Geeta.

Twins are born into a rich family. They get separated in their infancy. One continues in the same household, tormented by evil relatives. The other is raised by a poor family, becoming a daredevil. They grow up and get switched, causing immense confusion (for friends) and distress (to foes). This story is a big Hindi film favourite, with Dilip Kumar doing it in *Ram Aur Shyam* just a few years before *Seeta Aur Geeta*. It had been done even earlier as well. And yet, no one brought as much chutzpah to the double role as Hema Malini did in *Seeta Aur Geeta*. Her success meant the formula remained in vogue and several iterations were made with stars like Jeetendra, Anil Kapoor, Salman Khan, Varun Dhawan and – most memorably – Sridevi, all playing the double role.

Hema Malini got the role because Mumtaz, a top star then, quoted a fee unaffordable to the Sippys. Hema Malini was coming off another superhit – *Andaz* – with the same production house. The director and the writers were confident of her ability to play both roles – the fiery Geeta and the gentle Seeta – and took her on. To convince her, Ramesh Sippy told her that she'd probably win an award for her role. Which she did! Her only Best Actress Filmfare award was for *Seeta Aur Geeta*. Salim–Javed's script was fantastic, had great lines and played to her strengths – maybe even discovering her flair for physical comedy and comic timing for the first time. *Seeta Aur Geeta* is a rollicking film and is absolutely the type of entertainer that becomes a massive box-office hit. (Which also happened – it was the biggest grosser of the year.) But more than that, it established Hema Malini as the numero-uno heroine of the film industry, a mantle she wore for nearly a decade after that.

It also triggered something much bigger. *Seeta Aur Geeta* suddenly changed the dynamics of the hero-centric film industry, albeit temporarily. At a time when heroes were macho and were always expected to save damsels from distress, Hema Malini showed the villains their place as the twins. Even with the presence of a he-man like Dharmendra and an acclaimed actor like Sanjeev Kumar, it was Hema Malini who (literally) cracked the whip and called the shots. A fighting heroine was suddenly the new thing in town. When *Seeta Aur Geeta* released, a film called *Gehri Chaal* was being shot with Jeetendra and Amitabh Bachchan as the two heroes. But the makers modified the climax to have Hema Malini whip the villains for a bit. 'All of a sudden, she was the hero!' says Jeetendra about the heroine and the times.

Vijay Verma

Deewaar, 1975

The Naxal rebels of Bengal. Jayaprakash Narayan of Bihar. Bal Keshav Thackeray of Maharashtra. Siddhartha of Satyajit Ray's *Pratidwandi*. Shyam and Chhenu of *Mere Apne*. Birju of *Mother India*. Shambhu Mahto of *Do Bigha Zamin*. Terry Malloy of *On the Waterfront*.

Vijay Verma was the amalgamation of several characters and yet, he was nothing like any of them. He was helpless. He was wronged. He was a rebel. He took on the mighty for his rights. He was willing to break rules for what he believed were his rights. He refused to see himself as anything but right.

Many have noticed that the story of *Deewaar* was essentially the story of *Mother India* or *Ganga Jumna*, but that's selling the plot and characters way too short. For starters, the rural idyll of the earlier films had become an urban jungle. The main characters moved from one exploitative industrial labyrinth (a coal mine in, presumably, Jharkhand) to another (the construction sites and docks of Bombay). The professions, the language, the locations and the clothes had all become decidedly modern.

But what changed most from the earlier times was the scale of the injustice and the subsequent reaction. For his father's transgressions, Vijay received a tattoo '*Mera baap chor hai*' – an act of unimaginable violence without a drop of blood being shed. And that tattoo marked an indelible trauma on his soul. Unlike the earlier victims of Hindi cinema, who either remained mute (*Do Bigha Zamin*) or specifically went after their oppressors (*Mother India, Ganga Jumna*), Vijay Verma extracted his revenge from people who didn't oppress him but were replicas. He went after them with a vengeance hitherto unseen in Hindi cinema. And with tremendous amounts of swag.

Vijay's dockyard uniform with a knotted shirt. His *billa* number 786. His natty clothes, after striking big time. His cold fury. His measured drawl. His pithy lines – each one with the impact of a bullet. It was a perfect screenplay and a flawless performance. Not to mention, a magical box-office success. *Deewaar* struck such a chord with audiences that it ran endlessly – literally for years – in cinemas across the country. Its identification with the youth was so perfect all over India that three major stars – N.T. Rama Rao, Rajnikanth and Mammootty – appeared in the regional-language remakes.

Vijay Verma was not the first angry young man of Hindi cinema, but he was the most perfect embodiment of resentment and glamour, and this fixed this character in the collective consciousness of the nation. And replicas of this character carried on as the prime mover of Hindi cinema over three successive decades, making it the most durable of Hindi film formulas. Amitabh Bachchan himself, Vinod Khanna, Dharmendra, Mithun Chakraborty, Om Puri, Jackie Shroff, Anil Kapoor, Sunny Deol, Sanjay Dutt, Ajay Devgn and Shah Rukh Khan have all played versions of the angry young man – the rebel with a cause.

It took Amitabh Bachchan six years of struggle to land the role of Vijay Verma, which was then reprised for over two decades. Vijay was not called *lambi race ka ghoda* for nothing.

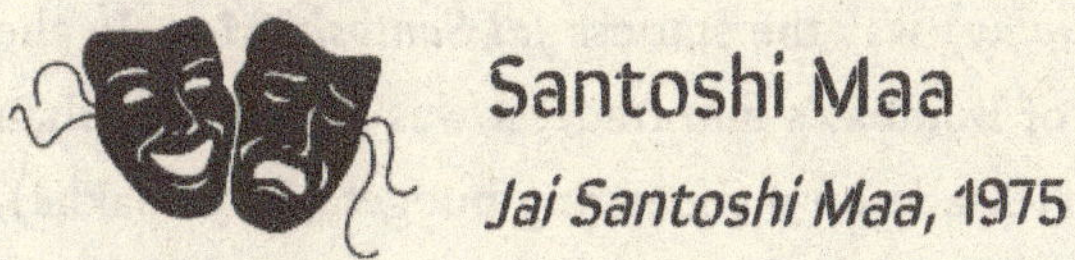

Santoshi Maa

Jai Santoshi Maa, 1975

When a family is separated in Manmohan Desai's megahit *Amar Akbar Anthony*, the mother leaves a letter for her husband and a talisman to protect him from harm. This talisman becomes a critical link in the chain of events that eventually unites the entire family two-and-a-half hours later. It is a locket of goddess Santoshi Maa.[5]

Hitmaker Manmohan Desai's films were the best barometer of public taste in the 1970s, and what he was capturing in his 1977 film was a trend that had caught on like wildfire after

5. Santoshi Maa popped up in the unlikeliest of places. In a Feluda novel by Satyajit Ray, a Bengali thriller writer laments that Bollywood is looking for devotional topics after the success of *Jai Santoshi Maa* and wonders aloud if a sequel – *Son of Santoshi* – would work!

the most surprising hit of 1975. In a year that had Amitabh Bachchan, Dharmendra, Hema Malini, Rajesh Khanna and Shashi Kapoor plying their trade, the second-biggest hit of the year (after *Sholay*) was the starless *Jai Santoshi Maa*. In the classification of Bombay's film trade, it was a bigger hit than even *Deewaar*! Made on a shoestring budget (Rs 25 lakhs), the distributors' investments were minuscule and the returns astronomical (it collected Rs 5 crore at the box office). *Jai Santoshi Maa* was yet another mythological movie, a genre that was the mainstay of the first few years of Hindi cinema. But for most of the 1960s and 1970s, mythological films were few and far between; they did decent business, but weren't among the biggest hits. People preferred romantic melodramas or action thrillers. *Jai Santoshi Maa* was the eye-popping outlier of this theory.

Jai Santoshi Maa is the story of Ganesha's daughter, Santoshi (Anita Guha) and her greatest devotee, Satyavati (Kanan Kaushal). The entire film is a series of misfortunes that befall Satyavati, orchestrated by the main goddesses of the Hindu pantheon, to test her devotion to Santoshi Maa. Of course, Santoshi Maa tries her best to protect her devotee from doom. The film put forth the concept of fasting and conducting a puja for 16 Fridays in Santoshi Maa's honour, which became popular all over India. The film was so well-received that cinema theatres were treated like temples as audiences entered barefoot and stood up whenever the goddess appeared on-screen, not to mention the real temples of the goddess that came up after the film.

The most plausible theory to explain *Jai Santoshi Maa*'s success is that the film was like a visual guide to worshipping to the goddess. Pujas for Santoshi Maa were gaining popularity in India since the 1960s, but the details were sketchy and not everyone could read the *vrat katha*. The film expanded on the 'life' of the goddess and provided details on conducting the puja. The main bhajan – '*Main toh aarti utaroo re Santoshi mata ki*' – became like an anthem for the puja, and continues to this day with original and remixed versions going from vinyl records to streaming services via cassettes and CDs.

Jai Santoshi Maa is a great example of the religious cult that cinema can bring to life and even embellish. Purely on the business from largely female and rural audiences, it managed to become an all-time blockbuster, creating an avalanche of copies and sequels, none of which were as successful. But it did hark to the market of devotional content, which would see a boom with Gulshan Kumar's T-Series churning out Vaishno Devi bhajans and selling cassettes in millions.

Gabbar Singh

Sholay, 1975

Abdul Rashid Khan, a Deputy Inspector General (DIG) of Central Provinces in pre-Independence India, had to contend with notorious dacoits in the deep ravines of Chambal, which came under his jurisdiction. DIG Khan used to tell stories of these dacoits to his son, Salim. One of the more dangerous ones used to cut off the ears and noses of policemen he captured. And the name of this dacoit stayed with young Salim – Gabbar Singh.

Javed Akhtar, as a young student, had travelled to Delhi for a youth festival in 1963. There, he watched a young actor in a play, and he made such an impact on him that Akhtar mentioned it several times to his writing partner. When looking for a villain in a major Hindi film they had written, they remembered this actor and recommended him to the director. The actor's name was Amjad Khan.

Like every iconic role, the influences go way back, and it is now impossible to separate Gabbar Singh from Amjad Khan. In the original scheme of things, Danny Denzongpa was supposed to play Gabbar. Given his intense style and unconventional looks, it could have been a memorable performance, but one cannot visualize the actor in any of *Sholay*'s scenes. Such was the impact of Amjad Khan on Gabbar.

The impact of Gabbar on the actor was equally strong. A newcomer when he was offered the role, he dug deep into himself to bring out the manic villainy to screen. He grew a beard, started living in army fatigues, started chewing tobacco and even coloured his teeth… All to get into character. Even when he was not shooting, he hung around the sets to assist the director and soak in the atmosphere. After some initial hiccups, he was so much into the character that even his co-stars felt his menace. While shooting the climax, he gripped Hema Malini's arm so ferociously that he left marks on her skin – not unlike how Gabbar would have treated Basanti.

The film fraternity wasn't impressed, though. His voice was considered weak, with several recommendations to dub it. He was not a big enough actor to match the three heroes of the film, everyone said. Except that the heroes themselves knew better… Amitabh Bachchan and Sanjeev Kumar both wanted to play Gabbar when they first heard the script. And the audience knew best. The menace of Gabbar spread through the audience like a narcotic, and they couldn't get enough of him. *Sholay* became the first Hindi film where the dialogues were so popular that 15 records were made of them and they outsold the song records. And the most popular record was *Gabbar Singh.*

It was a big risk to get there, though. Gabbar was nothing like what Hindi cinema had seen before. He was from a place 'between Uttar Pradesh and Mexico', Javed Akhtar once joked. His language was unusual, almost creating a new lingo. His lumbering body language was more intimidating than anything seen till then. And his actions were pure evil. He was the biggest risk of *Sholay*. He was also the most memorable thing about *Sholay.*

Over the years, the charm of Gabbar has increased… exponentially. Spoofs, parodies, tributes, jokes, graphic novels and advertisements have inundated us in the five decades since he first appeared on-screen. In the 1970s, Gabbar Singh was the first film character to endorse a product (Britannia Parle-G biscuits). In the 2000s, a version of Gabbar Singh was played by Amitabh Bachchan in a remake of *Sholay,* thus becoming a character who remained aspirational to the megastar for 30 years. Gabbar is unforgettable.

A villain as a brand endorser. Gabbar Singh (not Amjad Khan) starred in an advertisement campaign for Britannia Glucose D ads, a hit with children and families!

Image copyright: Britannia Industries Limited

Seth Deen Dayal, aka Lion

Kalicharan, 1976

A police officer discovers that the city's most-respected millionaire is actually a crime boss. In a typical filmi move, he proceeds to threaten the millionaire instead of reporting him, and is killed on the boss' orders. But before the next round of the game begins with a lookalike of the departed police officer, the confrontation scene with the millionaire is a masterclass in filmi villainy and has one of the most-repeated lines of Hindi cinema.

Ajit's career in villainy started after he found middling success as a hero in stunt films, often playing second fiddle to Dara Singh. His friend, Rajendra Kumar, offered the villain's role in *Suraj*, and Ajit started playing evil thakurs and princes, with nefarious designs on princely states or properties of rich but unsuspecting elderly. His turn as the suave, urban villain started with Prakash Mehra's *Zanjeer*. When writer Salim Khan was acting in small roles, he struck up a friendship with Ajit, and Salim–Javed wrote him the part for which he developed many of his signature traits. For starters, he developed a cool, almost languid style of speaking, because he had observed several mafia dons to realize that the truly powerful never spoke loudly or lost their temper. And a new brand of cool, calculating villain was born, who was perfect for the 1970s genre of baddies. After the money lender, dacoit and rich dad, we now had smugglers, black marketeers and crime bosses ruling the dens of evil. And Ajit was the man who brought all of that to life.

When Subhash Ghai wrote the script of *Kalicharan*, Ajit had already acted in hits like *Zanjeer*, *Jugnu* and *Yaadon Ki Baaraat* in his signature style. So, he gave a massive build-up to the character of Deen Dayal (who was being pitted against Shatrughan Sinha, once a top villain himself). Deen Dayal, aka Lion, was a cerebral villain, always a step ahead of the good guys. He is always well-dressed and well-accessorized, wearing sherwanis and using a desktop cigarette lighter to build his aura. And, of course, his accent – mispronouncing Lion as Loin – is now part of the Bollywood legend. His other characteristics – a moll called Mona (*Zanjeer*), a henchman called Robert (*Charas*)

– got built through a body of films, in a similar mould that went till the early 1980s.

Ajit got a new lease of life and developed something of a cult following in the 1990s for a truly 'different' reason. Actor Javed Jaffrey played a crime boss in an advertising campaign for Maggi Hot & Sweet Tomato Chilli Sauce, mimicking Ajit's tone and pronunciations. This led to the creation of an avalanche of over-the-top 'Ajit jokes' ('*Isse* liquid oxygen *mein daal do.* Liquid *isse jeene nahin dega aur* oxygen *isse marne nahin dega.*') that were in his voice but not necessarily from actual films. The trend got a further boost when Ajit's son, Shehzad Khan, played Bhalla in *Andaz Apna Apna* and spoke in his father's style to a sidekick he called Raabert. This wave – i.e. the first ad of the Maggi campaign – started with a line we all knew very well: '*Saara shaher mujhe* Loin *ke naam se jaanta hai...*'

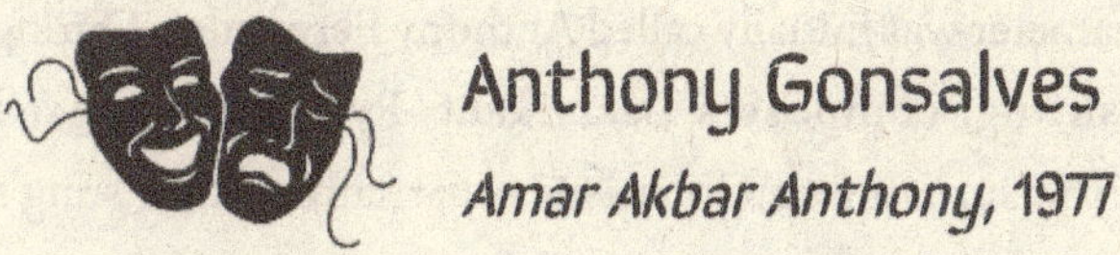

Anthony Gonsalves

Amar Akbar Anthony, 1977

In 1979, a girl had a severe fall and went into a coma at Bombay's Nanavati Hospital. In her coma, she kept mumbling 'Anthony'. It dawned on the doctor that it was Amitabh Bachchan's name in *Amar Akbar Anthony* and he contacted Bachchan. When the girl came out of her coma, she had her first mouthful of food from the superstar.

Anthony Gonsalves is the only character which has overshadowed Bachchan's actual name. Even Vijay – his most common character – was not as popular. Anthony also marked Bachchan's move from being the angry vigilante to a complete entertainer, who did action, dance, emotion and comedy with ease, and could fill theatres on his own. This complete package would diminish the need for every other type of performer in Hindi cinema and led to Bachchan being given the title of 'one-man industry'.

The character was initially called Anthony Fernandez. During a music sitting, composers Laxmikant–Pyarelal proposed changing the surname to Gonsalves – partially to fit a song's metre better and as tribute to one of the most respected music arrangers of the film industry, Anthony Gonsalves. The original Mr Gonsalves was called 'Maestro'. He was a big favourite of most composers, and is said to have taught Pyarelal how to play the violin.

The name came from Pyarelal. The lines came from Kader Khan, an ex-professor, who wrote the snappy street lingo Manmohan Desai loved. '*Aisa toh aadmi do-ich time bhaagta hai,* Olympic *ka* race *ho ya* police *ka case ho . . . ,*' drawls Anthony in one scene, ending his words with the distinctive '-ich' of Bombay slang.

Manmohan Desai gave Anthony all the mannerisms he had seen growing up in the lanes of Khetwadi area of Bombay. The director's inspiration, the real-life 'Anthony', ran an illicit hooch den right opposite his apartment and had a similar style of speaking. Both the actor and director worked in perfect sync, feeding off each other's ideas. Bachchan had this habit – from his college days – of mumbling gibberish from a Benjamin Disraeli speech. 'Sophisticated rhetorician intoxicated by his own verbosity' were the exact words, the sound of which Desai liked and put into the interludes of the '*My name is Anthony Gonsalves*' song!

For the famous drunken scene in front of the mirror, Desai explained the concept to Bachchan, and asked him to rehearse while he popped over to the next set in RK Studios to shoot a scene of *Parvarish* (which was on floors at the same time). In the time he was away, the scene was completed – Amitabh Bachchan giving 14 perfect takes, but due to some camera glitches, he had to give retakes. When Desai finally saw the rushes, he emotionally promised Bachchan that he would never make a film without him (and kept that promise).

It was the director and actor's first film together. When Desai first narrated the role to him, Bachchan expressed his reservations about the over-the-top character and the crazy nature of the script. Desai had replied, 'Lalla, after this film releases, people will not call you Amitabh. They will call you Anthony bhai!'

And the girl in Nanavati hospital proved him right.

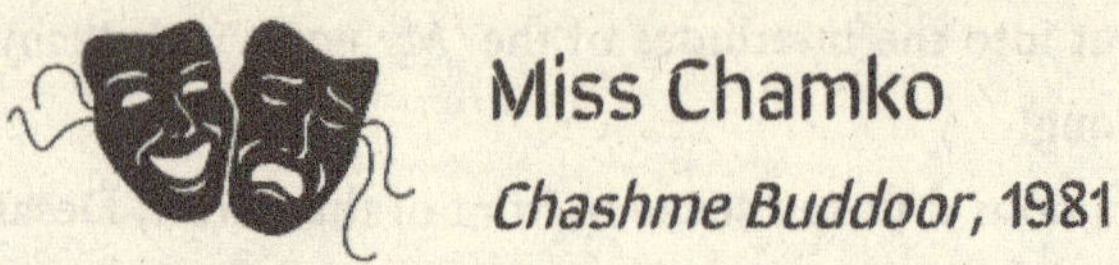

Miss Chamko

Chashme Buddoor, 1981

Imagine you are living in a Delhi *barsaati*, studying at the university. You have never spoken to a girl outside of your family. You are the studious kind, but hope to have that special someone in your life. Someone special enough to make you give up smoking – only if she asks once, with a special smile. Someone you can take to the Talkatora Gardens for Tutti Frutti. Someone who loves classical music. Loves it enough to go to Sargam Sangeet Vidyalay twice a week for lessons. Loves it enough to go door to door selling detergent powder, raising money for the fees.

Neha Rajan was that girl. And you were, we all were, Siddharth Parashar. Everything about *Chashme Buddoor* had an old-world charm around it, along with a sheen of fantasy. The city of Delhi was spacious, misty and had an air of wistfulness about it. Outstation students could afford to live in large quarters, though the last few days before the 'money order' came through were brutal. Roadside Romeos weren't aggressive or violent – they were almost benign. Even the gang kidnapping girls for ransom seemed to be a bumbling bunch with no deviant tendencies. And nothing exemplifies this better than Deepti Naval's character – the delightfully frothy Miss Chamko – who earned her pocket money by selling detergent door to door, despite coming from an upper middle-class background.

Deepti Naval's character was the culmination of several years of very real and lovable women characters in parallel Hindi cinema. It started with Vidya Sinha in *Rajnigandha* and *Chhoti Si Baat* in the mid-1970s, and picked up steam in the late 1970s and early 1980s. Bindiya Goswami in *Gol Maal*, Swaroop Sampat in *Naram Garam* were beautiful as the girls next door, getting caught up in their boyfriends' crazy capers and yet, maintaining a character of their own. Deepti Naval was exemplary in this type of role – her bright smile lighting up the lives of people around her in *Saath, Kissi Se Na Kehna, Katha, Rang Birangi* and of course *Chashme Buddoor*. A great indicator of the popularity of this type of character was that even top stars like Rekha

(*Khubsoorat*) and Parveen Babi (*Rang Birangi*) played roles like this to great popularity and acclaim. And her name in the movie, Neha (suggested by lyricist Indu Jain), became a popular name. Director Sai Paranjpye recalls several goddaughters called Neha, all of who were born in the early 1980s.

Farooq Sheikh – with his easy charm and smooth demeanour – was just the perfect foil for her. They were made for each other. An independent woman who finds happiness in a mild-mannered and easy-going man is still the stuff middle-class romantic dreams are made of. Neha singing '*Kaali ghodi pe gora sainyan*' at a Delhi bus stop would have been incomplete without Farooq Sheikh on his black motorcycle. And both of them reciting the cliché-ridden advertising jingle that never turns old: '*Kapdon ke liye behtareen sabun, baar lagataar, kapdon mein chakachaundh chamak lane ke liye, khushboodar jhaagwala... Chamko!*'

Kavita Sanyal

Arth, 1982

On a trip to London, Mahesh Bhatt woke up one night in the plush apartment he was staying in with his companion, Parveen Babi. He went out to the living room and found Parveen sitting near a lamp, staring at her palm. 'This became her defining image for me,' he says while describing the character of Kavita Sanyal in his defining film, *Arth*.

Mahesh Bhatt's brand of film-making has been described as 'relationship porn'. In many of his movies, he has shown his relationships in brutal detail, and tried to reach a catharsis by 'digging into [his] own wounds'. *Arth* was his breakthrough film. It was a sleeper hit, received critical acclaim and laid his life bare. The story of a volatile film-maker (Kulbhushan Kharbanda) falling in love with a mentally ill actress, Kavita (Smita Patil), and walking out of his marriage was straight out of his love story with Parveen Babi. While *Arth* is the wife's story, Kavita's character was entirely modelled on Parveen. The wife, Pooja (Shabana Azmi), also took several elements from Mahesh Bhatt's first wife, Lorraine Bright (who had changed her name to Kiran Bhatt).

When Mahesh Bhatt met Parveen after her affair with Kabir Bedi ended, she was a star with several superhits to her credit while he was a newcomer director. When they began seeing each other, Parveen insisted that he move in with her. Which he did, after abandoning his wife and children. He tagged along with Parveen for a European holiday, staying in swanky apartments that she paid for. During this trip, her spiritual guru, U.G. Krishnamurti, had joked about the fate line on her palm and Parveen became obsessed with it. Leading to the image of her staring at her palm.

Kavita Sanyal is one of the very few instances of a real, living person receiving such an unabashedly negative portrayal in a film. Her generosity (of funding her lover's marital home) is counterpointed by her insistence that he first abandons and then divorces his helpless wife. Mahesh Bhatt doesn't let himself off the hook either. He was unable to cope with the pressures of Parveen's mental illness, as well as having to navigate his way in a household run by her mother. He eventually slid out of the relationship – as shown in the film – and later admitted to his cowardice and immaturity.

Kavita Sanyal – played by Smita Patil with a manic edge – is a short but unforgettable role. When Shabana Azmi walked away with all the awards for her author-backed role, Smita Patil was very disappointed and even stopped talking to Bhatt. But her searing portrayal laid bare all the secrets around Parveen's illness, and – many say – precipitated her final escape from Bollywood at the peak of her stardom. During the making and after its release, Parveen Babi was constantly asked about *Arth* – a very troubling experience because some of her most vulnerable moments were up there for the world to see. Her outward pride at Mahesh's success would have come at the cost of intense internal turmoil. As the song went, '*Tum itna jo muskura rahe ho, kya gham hai jisko chhupa rahe ho…*'

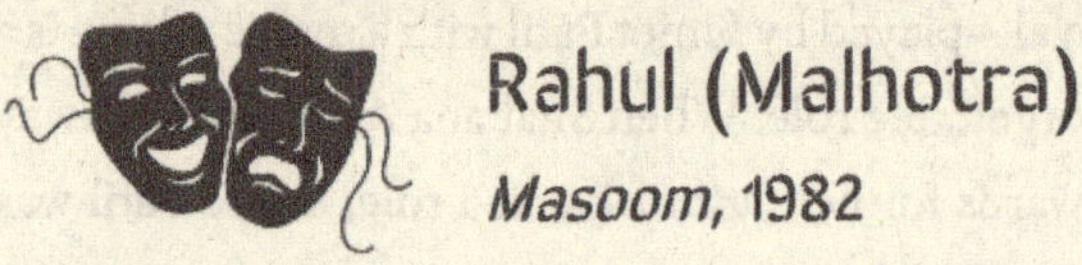

Rahul (Malhotra)

Masoom, 1982

When *Masoom* released, many families took their children to watch the film – where infidelity and illegitimacy are key themes – probably seeing a little boy dominating the posters and hearing about the children's songs in the film. Naseeruddin Shah has a wicked explanation for this. 'Everybody showed their children *Masoom*. To prepare the ground, I guess,' he deadpans.

Based on Erich Segal's novel *Man, Woman and Child*, *Masoom* is one of those rare instances where the film surpasses the source material. The story is about a little boy, Rahul (Jugal Hansraj), suddenly thrust into an architect, DK's (Naseeruddin Shah) happy family. The child was born out of a one-night stand the architect had had 10 years ago. The boy's mother – who had kept it a secret – had just passed away, and the boy must now live with DK's family.

Director Shekhar Kapur told the basic plot of *Man, Woman and Child* to Gulzar, and the writer wrote the screenplay without reading the novel, while staying in Bangalore's Taj West End hotel during a summer holiday. After Kapur heard the screenplay, he said 'Gulzar sahab, *mera khayal hai ab aap* novel *mat padhiyega.*'

One of the major departures from the novel was that the main character of the little boy has less choice in the matter and, yet, packs a far bigger emotional wallop. Jugal Hansraj – who played Rahul – was seen in an advertisement by Shekhar Kapur and offered the role. His awareness of the role's predicament was limited, but Kapur is an excellent director of children, and the child actor's innocence melted everyone. His chemistry with his two stepsisters – played by Urmila Matondkar and Aradhana Srivastav – brought a smile to our faces, while his anchorless existence wreaked havoc with our hearts.

'*Main tumhari* mummy *nahin hoon*': This sharp retort by Shabana Azmi – playing Shah's wife – pretty much encapsulates the dilemma of a married woman having to confront her husband's infidelity. The triumph of *Masoom* comes because no one – the errant husband, the angry wife, the other woman and, least of all, the little boy – is at fault. They are victims of circumstance, trying to fit into roles they didn't choose themselves. They are not angry with life, just perplexed.

For children, *Masoom* is a fun ride, with Jugal Hansraj and the two girls providing entertainment, including the definitive children's song '*Lakdi ki kathi, kathi pe ghoda*'. For adults, it is a grim realization of the responsibilities we sometimes take on unwillingly but end up defining us. In a poignant scene, the father looks at the son's drawing and asks, '*Aapke* papa *chashma pehente hain?*' And when the boy says yes, he quietly takes off his glasses. *Masoom* is an exceptionally durable film that was with us when we were Rahul and remains when we might be DK. Or, as film critic Harneet Singh writes, '*Masoom* had everything for everyone. It's a film that grows old with you — those who sang *Lakdi ki kathi* now sing *Tujhse naaraz nahin zindagi*.'

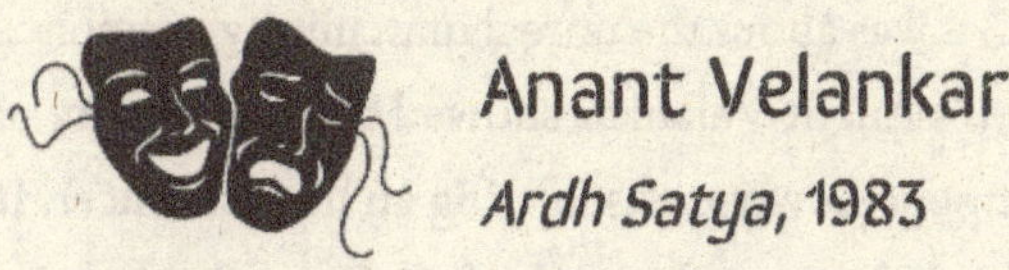

Anant Velankar

Ardh Satya, 1983

Ek palde mein napunsakta / Ek palde mein paurush,
Aur theek tarazu ke kaante par / Ardh satya.

– From Dilip Chitre's poem *Ardh Satya*

Towards the end of *Ardh Satya*, Anant Velankar (Om Puri) breaks down, and his friend, Jyotsna (Smita Patil), reaches forward to take his hand and console him. But she stops just short. This exact movement was taken from a rehearsal, when Om Puri was reading the above poem, which epitomized the film's theme. Now, as a politically aware and sensitive person, he started weeping. Director Govind Nihalani started to comfort him, but realized a mere touch would not provide enough solace for his anguish.

If *Zanjeer*'s Vijay Khanna – made famous by Amitabh Bachchan in 1973 – was about the unreal masculinity of a police officer, *Ardh Satya*'s Anant Velankar showed the grim reality of the police department slowly emasculating an honest officer. It merged a Marathi short story *Surya* (by S.D. Panvalkar) about a wife-beating police officer forcing his son to join the police force and the theme of Dilip Chitre's poem – the helplessness of an individual against the system.

To bring the role to life, Om Puri learnt to ride a bike and worked on his body by joining the newly opened gym at Holiday Inn hotel. He also spent time with police officers at Mahim and Girgaum stations – even witnessing the interrogation of a real suspect. The movie was so real that the scenes between Velankar and his father (Amrish Puri) in the film greatly disturbed Om Puri's actual father, reminding him of his own patriarchal behaviour towards his family.

Om Puri's portrayal of the honest but cornered police officer up against a mafia don (Sadashiv Amrapurkar) had the added subtext of a Maharashtrian locking horns with a South Indian don – something that found resonance with the popular sentiment in Bombay of the time. His performance was universally appreciated (including winning a National Award for Best Actor) and the film did quite well commercially, running for 22 weeks in Bombay and competing against blockbusters like *Coolie*. It also got Om Puri noticed as an acting powerhouse, even by commercial film-makers.

Twenty years later, Om Puri was shooting with Amitabh Bachchan for Govind Nihalani's *Dev*. During the shoot, he thanked Bachchan because apparently the superstar had refused *Ardh Satya* for lack of dates. Bachchan himself had no recollection of this, but he did meet Nihalani after *Ardh Satya*, expressing his desire to work with him. That script took two decades to come into being, and it became *Dev*, in which Bachchan played an upright officer taking on the system. And Om Puri played a corrupt officer – a pliant tool in the hands of the political administration. In the intervening 20 years, Anant Velankar's delicate balance had settled in the favour of *napunsakta*.

The Mahabharata Ensemble

Jaane Bhi Do Yaaro, 1983

'*Draupadi tere akele ki nahin hai. Hum sab* shareholder *hain!*' A goggled and slightly drunk Bheem snarls to Yudhishthir, and millions of people, watching Doordarshan, all over the country laughed their guts out – thus, the cult of *Jaane Bhi Do Yaaro* took shape. 'An abiding memory from those drawing-room viewings is of everyone waiting for the Mahabharata scene to begin: it was the ultimate pay-off, a cultural touchstone for our generation,' says Jai Arjun Singh in his seminal book on *Jaane Bhi Do Yaaro*.

Director Kundan Shah had conceived of a rather tame sequence as the climax in the first draft of the script, in which the two photographers are tricked into handing over all the incriminating proof they have against the unscrupulous builder, Tarneja. Once the co-writers, Ranjit Kapoor and Satish Kaushik, came on board, they came up with the idea of having all the main characters getting mixed up in a stage play. They wanted a well-recognized play to transplant their characters into and after considering *Laila Majnu,* they decided on Mahabharata – specifically the scene where Draupadi is disrobed. The idea was to heighten the comedy using the Sankritized Hindi usually associated with the Mahabharata ('*Shaant, gadadhaari* Bheem, *shaant!*') and the large number of characters to which they added Drupad ('*Nalayak. Adharmi. Durachari. Bhamachari* [sic]. *Bhrashtachari. Bol* sorry.') and even Emperor Akbar ("This is too much. *Yeh* Akbar *kahan se aa tapka?*').

And, in keeping with the satirical tone of the film, all the conventional roles were reversed. Duryodhan and Dushshasan (played by Naseeruddin Shah and Ravi Baswani[6]) were preventing the disrobing of Draupadi (played by Satish Shah, as a corpse), while the Pandavas (Om Puri as Bheem and Pankaj Kapoor as Drupad) wanted to take off with her. The

6. The original Dushshasan was played by Vidhu Vinod Chopra, who was the production controller of the film. The junior artiste selected for the role suddenly asked for a much higher fee on the day of the shoot and Chopra decided to step in to keep the budget in check.

Mahabharata scene comprised almost all the main characters of *Jaane Bhi Do Yaaro*, many of whom were originally stage actors (trained in the National School of Drama [NSD]) and brought a manic edge to the scene.

The film took a long time in the making and a limited release happened almost by accident. But the impact was immediate. Someone told the team: 'There was so much laughter during the Mahabharata scene that people could have got a heart attack', which was the first external feedback received. Despite several technical glitches, the impact of the scene and the film was terrific. On pure word of mouth alone and good reviews, *Jaane Bhi Do Yaaro* ran for 37 weeks in Delhi, in the morning show in a few smaller halls. And then of course, Doordarshan took over.

The rampant hilarity of the scene got a boost because of the brutal, cynical ending that followed immediately afterwards. And it is telling about Indian democracy that both the hilarious Mahabharata sequence and the serious ending have remained topical over the last four decades. As Dhritarashtra had asked plaintively in the movie, '*Beta,* Duryodhan, *yeh sab kya ho raha hai?*'

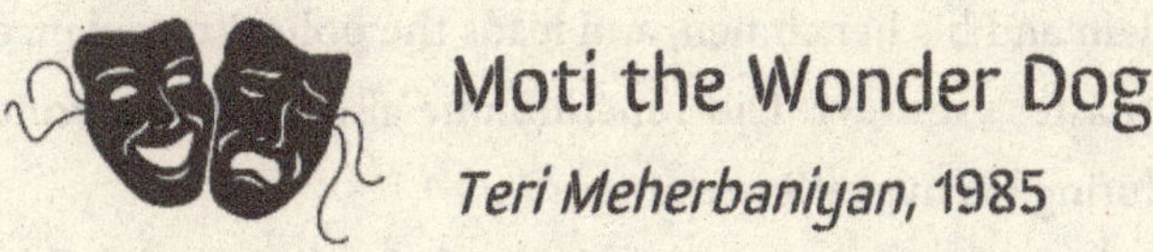

Moti the Wonder Dog

Teri Meherbaniyan, 1985

A young man comes to a village ruled by tyrant zamindar. He rebels against the zamindar and falls in love with a girl. The zamindar has an eye on the girl and he tries to rape her. The girl commits suicide and the zamindar has the young man killed. A member of his family performs their last rites and decides to take revenge against the zamindar.

Ho-hum ... This is such a Bollywood cliché.

Now, wait a minute ... What if I told you the family member who takes revenge is a dog?

speechless

Teri Meherbaniyan had an A-list lead pair (Jackie Shroff and Poonam Dhillon), but decided to bet on a dog to be the provider of vigilante justice. To the plaintive tune of '*Teri meherbaniyan, teri kadardaniya*', the dog is part of his master's funeral procession, performs his last rites as per Hindu customs, kills the villain and his henchmen, and leads the police to evidence of his master's murder. Did I mention he also sheds glycerine tears during his master's memorial?

But then Moti, aka Brownie, was a 'Wonder Dog' and in peak demand for his skills. Moti had starred in the original Kannada version of *Teri Meherbaniyan* and became a national star soon after. He was in *Mard* as Amitabh Bachchan's faithful companion, and helped the superstar in his fight against the British.[7] For a fight scene in *Mard*, Bachchan enters an exclusive club and proceeds to smash the 'Dogs and Indians not allowed' signboard to smithereens – with active support from Moti, even getting a mention in the title song. Director Manmohan Desai gushed, 'He is the most fantastic dog I have ever seen. It is unbelievable the way he does exactly what you want without any retakes.'

Moti was a star in his own right and (his owner) charged a fee between Rs 1–2 lakh per film (in the mid-1980s). If you

---

7. Director Manmohan Desai had said that Bachchan's character in *Mard* 'was nothing but [comic book superhero] Phantom', a superhero with a horse and dog (actually, a wolf) to help him.

thought this was a bit much, there were several film-makers who had to settle for other dogs because getting Moti's dates was a major problem. The owner–dog team insisted on air-conditioned rooms whenever they travelled for shoots, and this dog was every inch the star!

Animals in Hindi films have covered the entire gamut – from elephants (*Haathi Mere Saathi*) to cows (*Gaai Aur Gori*) to horses (*Sholay*) to snakes (innumerable). There was a significant number of films starring dogs, from the mid-80s to the mid-90s, many of them inspired by the success of Moti. Be it the detective dog in *Bol Radha Bol* or the stand-in mother in *Maa*, there were an entire sub-genre of films that depended on the dog as the prime mover. This reached a crescendo when the climax of Hindi cinema's biggest hit – *Hum Aapke Hain Koun..!* – was decided by a dog. From the contributions of Dhanno in *Sholay*, we now had Tuffy – something of a spiritual descendant of Moti!

Mogambo

Mr India, 1987

'*Mogambo khush hua!*'

When newbie director Shekhar Kapur asked his scriptwriter, Javed Akhtar, to explain the character of this mega-villain, he got these three words in response. Hiding his exasperation, Kapur asked him to explain further. 'Shekhar sahab, [after this film releases] when Kapil Dev hits a sixer, people will shout "*Mogambo khush hua*". When people get three aces in a game of *teen patti*, they will say "*Mogambo khush hua*". You trust me on that!'

Akhtar wrote the character of a megalomaniac who uses verbal approval to reward his gang and – according to Kapur – it fit perfectly with the comic-book pitch of the film. Here was a villain who had an island hideout off the coast of India, wanted to fan tensions between India's diverse groups, made money off adulteration of food, but ultimately got beaten up by a rag-tag bunch of kids led by a violinist. Kapur said, '[Mogambo was] bloodthirsty only in intention, but never in action.'

Amrish Puri was on a high, even before *Mr India* came along. He was a leading villain of Bollywood. He had even been to Hollywood (*Indiana Jones and the Temple of Doom*), where Steven Spielberg praised him as 'my favourite villain – the best the world has ever produced and ever will!' It was a tall order to go higher up than this, but Amrish Puri managed to do just that with Mogambo – often called the second most memorable villain of Hindi cinema (right after Gabbar Singh, also created by Salim–Javed). It is also easily his most memorable. If Javed Akhtar's explanation to Kapur was unconventional, Kapur's direction to Puri was even more so! 'Imagine you are playing Shakespeare to nine-year-old kids and they have no idea who he was. Imagine you have to make it feel mythic and entertaining.' A consummate stage actor, Puri hit this brief perfectly and brought a deliciously devilish dimension to the role.

The writing and the performance were accentuated by the costume (which is now a favourite at all Bollywood theme parties), the grand set (complete with a throne, an acid tank and a map of India at his feet) and the sound design (the exaggerated clicking of his rings on a globe placed on his throne). There was a whole choreography behind all the times Mogambo said those three magic words – creating a balance between predictability (he's going to say it again!) and surprise (but how?).

During the final editing, Kapur wanted to reduce the number of times Mogambo says his iconic line, but Javed Akhtar insisted that the number of times it was said was part of the character's charm and would increase the repeat value of the film. About a year after *Mr India* released, Shekhar Kapur was in Sharjah for a cricket match. Kapil Dev hit a six. And a banner went up: '*Mogambo khush hua!*' Javed Akhtar's words had come true.

Mahesh Deshmukh, urf Munna

Tezaab, 1988

A biker gang attacks a rocking dance show in a crowded maze of lanes. They kidnap the lead dancer and escape. A young girl witnesses the mayhem and sends off a telegram to her brother – a criminal expelled from the city. He cuts his vigilantism in another city short to return. Meanwhile, a police officer surveys the damage at the dance show and is intrigued when he sees the photo of the expelled criminal. He wants to know, '*Yeh* Mahesh Deshmukh *se* Munna *kaise ban gaya?*' Anil Kapoor's stardom was the story of him going from a boy next door (*Woh 7 Din, Saaheb, Chameli Ki Shaadi*) to a lovable rogue (*Andar Baahar, Karma*) to an unlikely superhero (*Mr India*), till he hit the big time as Munna.

For starters, Anil Kapoor got the role after some hectic lobbying by his brother Boney Kapoor. Director N. Chandra was originally an editor, who started his career with Boney Kapoor's home production, *Woh 7 Din*. Boney Kapoor saw the potential of *Tezaab*'s script and ensured his brother got the role by adjusting his shooting dates for other films. Anil Kapoor made the role of the navy cadet turned gangster his own, winning a Filmfare Award for Best Actor in the process. Bollywood had taken to the grungy look, the *tapori* style and the swaggering body language earlier, but it reached peak popularity with Anil Kapoor. It also became the actor's signature role.

Tezaab was N. Chandra's third film and his biggest hit. He had started a formula with his first two films – *Ankush* and *Pratighaat* – that reached a commercial crescendo with *Tezaab*. The formula was about the struggles of Maharashtra's educated and unemployed youth – much of it against 'outsiders', who seem to be oppressing them or taking away opportunities. The youth against a corrupt system was a popular theme in the 1980s, with police officers and politicians presented as the key villains. Sunny Deol in *Arjun* and Anil Kapoor himself in *Mashaal* were such characters – both films becoming big hits.

N. Chandra was said to have brought 'dirty realism' into commercial Hindi cinema. But after seeing two low-budget successes, *Tezaab* was scaled on to a bigger canvas, and the character of Mahesh Deshmukh was the right mixture of realism and glamour. He was up against an army of very formidable villains – Lotiya Pathan (Kiran Kumar), Shyamlal (Anupam Kher), Inspector Gupta (Mahavir Shah) and Mukut Bihari (Jack Gaud) – that made his character much bigger and memorable than those from N. Chandra's earlier films.

Tezaab's action scenes were bigger, the music caught the nation's imagination, and the dialogues were legendary. Ex-adman Kamlesh Pandey wrote lines that were pure adrenaline and suited Anil Kapoor's style of dialogue delivery really well. His first appearance in the film was literally on the edge of a knife when he told a roadside goon, '*Tere zindagi aur maut ke beech ka faasla* Munna *ke chaku ki dhaar se zyada nahin hai.*' It was a dynamite entrance and role, the type that makes careers. It certainly made Anil Kapoor's.

Chandni

Chandni, 1989

'How can you have Vinod Khanna and no action?' asked a distributor, who walked out of a trial show of *Chandni*. Yash Chopra was 'sick of violence', and rewrote the first half of the film – after starting the shoot – to make it more romantic and musical. He had moved to multi-starrer potboilers – *Mashaal, Faasle, Vijay* – after his last romantic film (*Silsila*) didn't do well, despite a top-notch star cast. But now he had had enough and, with *Chandni,* he – along with youngsters Mansoor Khan and Sooraj Barjatya – introduced a new wave of romance that swept Hindi cinema.

Chandni was Rekha's name in *Silsila* and she was the first choice for the role when Chopra conceived the story. Sridevi, who was fast becoming big in Bollywood, came in later and, at that time, she still wasn't very familiar with Hindi and assistants had to explain the lines to her. None of that is visible in her assured performance though, which ran the entire gamut of essentials that a Hindi film demands. She does comedy. She emotes. She dances like a dream. She even sang a song ('*Chandni o meri Chandni*') in an album that went on to become the bestseller of the decade.

Yash Chopra's biographer, Rachel Dwyer, wrote, 'Chandni is an ideal woman, seen through the eyes of her two lovers.' It was a heroine-centric film, featuring Sridevi as a bubbly young girl, a serious career woman (a rarity in Bollywood) and, finally, as a mature lover.

Chandni was an ode to Sridevi. Rohit (Rishi Kapoor) covers gigantic walls in his room with Chandni's photographs. He showers petals on her from a helicopter. He cures himself from paralysis to get back with her. Lalit (Vinod Khanna) – her next lover – forgets his previous romance when he sees Chandni. She was the epitome of womanhood, as envisaged by Yash Chopra who was soon to be called 'King of Romance'. Sridevi got a totally new look – made of whites and pastels – by Bhanu Athaiya and Leena Daru. It created a nationwide craze as the '*Chandni* look', and spawned many clones.

Sridevi was on the ascendance when she did *Chandni*. Her first hit, *Himmatwala*, and several others with South Indian film-makers had given her a foothold in the industry, but not respectability. There had been jokes about her 'thunder thighs' and her accent. By 1987, she had done projects with most of the big banners and had delivered major hits like *Nagina* and *Mr India*. By 1989, she was a huge star in her own right. *Nigahen*, the sequel of *Nagina*, was made and sold on her name alone and, in *Chaalbaaz*, she overshadowed superstars like Sunny Deol and Rajinikanth. But after *Chandni*'s success, she became an iconic heroine – one for the ages. And the distributors had a new name for her that also explained the film's success – you can get away with Vinod Khanna not doing action when you have the 'female Amitabh Bachchan' in the film.

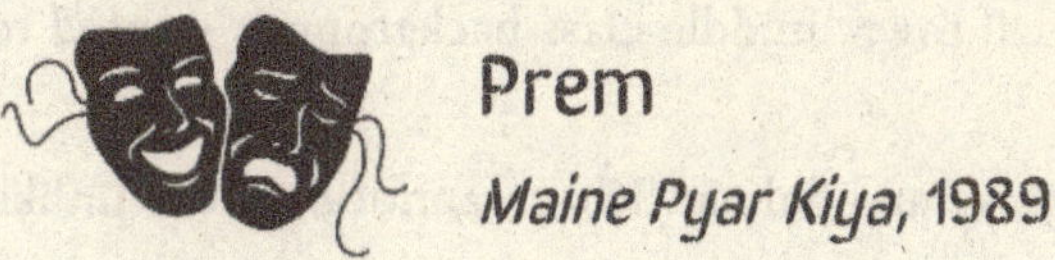

Prem

Maine Pyar Kiya, 1989

'*Bade* old-fashioned *ho,* Prem!' says the 'modern woman'. She is taunting a millionaire's heir as the 'homely woman' dutifully cleans the mess the former has created.

If there ever was a moment that explains the quintessential Barjatya hero, it was this. In his very first film, Sooraj Barjatya named his hero, defined his character and didn't change any of it for the next 30 years (and counting). For any other director, 'old fashioned' would have been an insult. For Barjatya, it's a badge of honour.

The director confessed in a later interview that Prem was basically him. From *Maine Pyar Kiya* to *Hum Aapke Hain Koun..!* to *Hum Saath-Saath Hain,* the progression of the character –

from a brat to a more emotional, mature man – was Sooraj Barjatya himself evolving. Or rather, it was the character that Sooraj Barjatya and – according to him – countless shy Indian boys, from small town, middle-class backgrounds wanted to become.

Sooraj Barjatya and Salman Khan cannot be more unlike one another in real life. And yet, their careers got intertwined right from the beginning. They started together with *Maine Pyar Kiya* – both in their early twenties when they began filming. They both faced scepticism from the industry, with even newcomers refusing to star as the heroine in the movie. But they persisted with each other, making mistakes, finding their feet and being loyal to one another. Salman's voice was considered to be too 'light' and industry folks recommended that it be dubbed by someone else. Sooraj ignored them and simply asked Salman to redub in the afternoons, when his voice sounded a bit heavier. He was, in a way, backing himself.

Prem was the perfect mix of sexy and *sanskari*. He studied abroad, but came back to join the family business. He wore bomber jackets, but touched everyone's feet dutifully. He started smoking abroad, but gave it up when a 'friend' asked him to. He was a softy, but could throw a mean punch when pushed to. He wanted to marry a girl who wore miniskirts (and had a cool mom to talk about it), but it was all play-acting. He was respectful towards his father, but willing to walk out for the woman he loved. He was the person you could depend on for doing the right thing. And helping the family out of a spot... Especially when the bride's family stole the groom's slippers!

Prem was essentially the same character that turned more responsible in *Hum Aapke Hain Koun..!* His impetuousness hadn't reduced, only his loyalty to the family came to the fore. With *Hum Saath-Saath Hain,* Prem had transformed into an even more dutiful and thoughtful person. Salman Khan wanted to do the role eventually played by Saif Ali Khan, a more playful character – in line with his screen image. But Sooraj Barjatya saw Salman only as the bookworm – the soft-spoken Prem. Even in films that didn't have Salman Khan (*Vivah,* for example), the Barjatya hero was always named Prem and it was always the same guy who closed his eyes when applying ointment on an injured girl's legs.

Vijay Dinanath Chauhan

Agneepath, 1990

'*Chhattees saal, nau mahine, aath din, yeh solva ghanta chalu hai.*' When Amitabh Bachchan rasped out his first lines in *Agneepath*, the customary whistles and coins that accompanied his first dialogue in a film almost screeched to a halt. Vijay Dinanath Chauhan was a Hindi film hero like nobody had seen – or heard – before.

For starters, this was the first time a mainstream commercial film had a middle-aged hero. In an industry where 40-something heroes hang around colleges to woo women half their age, or seamlessly transition to 70-something patriarchs, a 37-year-old mafia don was certainly a novelty. And it was also the first time since *Reshma Aur Shera* that Amitabh Bachchan didn't speak in his signature baritone. He created a rasping voice for the character, modelling it on the voice of Tamilian don Varadarajan Mudaliar. It created such a backlash that the film had to be redubbed with his original voice after the first week.

Vijay is the son of village schoolteacher, Dinanath Chauhan, affectionately known as 'Masterji'. Masterji is framed and lynched because he tries to stop the entry of evil into the village. Young Vijay doesn't find a single helping hand in the village and single-handedly drags his father's body for his cremation. The resulting strain on his vocal chords leads to him developing his signature rasp. Vijay leaves the village with his mother and sister, and reaches Bombay. His daredevilry earns him a job with four underworld dons and he grows up to become a Robin Hood–like character, who takes control of the Bombay underworld and locks horns with international crime boss, Kancha Cheena.

This much-used plot became a cult classic – thanks to Kader Khan's explosive dialogues, one amazing poem by Harivansh Rai Bachchan and Bachchan's god-level delivery of both. It was embellished by a masterful build-up of Vijay Chauhan's mythos among his people. While the film was said to be inspired by the Al Pacino–starrer, *Scarface,* it was more of an extension of the original Bachchan mythology – made famous in films like *Deewaar* and *Shakti.* The anti-hero rising from the streets, polishing shoes, punching above his weight, escaping death, finding unconventional love, and losing his principled mother's love were all part of the anti-hero's story in *Deewaar*. *Agneepath* was grittier, its canvas much grander and the hero more jaded (not to mention, older) than the earlier films.

All this didn't work. *Agneepath* flopped. Despite a National Award for Amitabh Bachchan, audiences didn't 'get' his voice (which was thought to be an audio glitch in many places) or the character. Two decades later, Dharma Productions remade the film on a more violent and flashy scale – which turned out to be a big hit. This was literally the best of both worlds. Fans of Amitabh Bachchan had a cult classic. Fans of Hrithik Roshan had an entertainer. And Vijay. Dinanath. Chauhan. lived. on.

Amitabh Bachchan as Vijay Chavan, the don whose voice, family and body all came under attack. But he stood gloriously tall.

Under license by Dharma Productions Private Limited

Maharani

Sadak, 1991

The Marathi play, *Bhatala Dili Osari*, is about a character called Kinchit Gandharva – a male actor playing female roles on stage and developing an effeminate manner even in real life. Written in 1956, it was a popular comedy performed across Maharashtra by professional theatre companies as well as college groups. One such production was in the University of Pune, starring a young student called Sadashiv Amrapurkar.

Amrapurkar used this character as a reference for his landmark role of '*Jism ke* bazaar *ka* maharaja – *Maharani*' in Mahesh Bhatt's *Sadak*. The non-binary brothel-keeper was developed after an input from Sanjay Dutt from his days as a drug addict when he came across a slumlord who dressed as a woman and still managed to boss everyone around. Maharani – despite her over-the-top mannerisms – has a clear character arc described through her dialogues. She was abandoned by her family after her sexuality was revealed, and ended up becoming a sex worker and then a madam. As a brothel-keeper, she is cunning, powerful and ruthless.

Her '*aadha mard, aadhi aurat*' sexuality is brought out in two scenes, where she dresses up as a woman in the first and shaves herself in the second. And her villainous depravity comes out in multiple scenes starting from when she convinces a sex worker's (Soni Razdan) conservative family to abandon her because of the sexually transmitted disease she has contracted. When a lover (Sanjay Dutt) of one of her girls (Pooja Bhatt) comes up with a plan to elope, Maharani subtly scuttles the plan by keeping one of his friends (Deepak Tijori) hostage. She has informers in the police, she ruthlessly puts down her enemies and is an understated menace. Several quirks of Maharani's character also didn't make it to the final cut. Amrapurkar said later that the character would toss a coin in front of her pooja room to decide her dominant sexuality for the day. She is cruel to everyone except the crippled old man in front of her brothel because she knows she could also end up like this someday. The conventional Bollywood wisdom – to maintain an unrelenting focus on the lead pair – kept these scenes out.

Sadak suffered as a film because of the assembly-line style of film-making in 1990s Bollywood. Pooja Bhatt's blow-dried hair and posh make-up are completely at odds with her supposed background as a village girl. Despite this shoddiness, *Sadak* was one of the biggest hits of the year, buoyed by a superhit soundtrack by Nadeem–Shravan. But the real star of the film was Sadashiv Amrapurkar.

There's an adage that says that whenever something makes an impact in Bollywood, Filmfare institutes an award for it. Maharani was impactful enough for Filmfare Awards to start a category for the Best Performance in a Negative Role in that year – which Sadashiv Amrapurkar duly won.

Ajay Sharma/Vicky Malhotra

Baazigar, 1993

Zoya Akhtar's *Luck by Chance* is set around the making of a film – *Dil Ki Aag* – starring a newcomer. The story of the film within the film is about a 'negative character', who murders the heroine's sister. If there was any doubt about what this story resembled, it was dispelled when Karan Johar appeared (playing himself) and reminded us that every time a superstar has turned down an unconventional role, a newcomer has quickly filled his shoes. Seven stars left *Zanjeer* to make way for Amitabh Bachchan, he reminded us. And many stars left *Baazigar*, which gave us Shah Rukh Khan.

Baazigar – adapted from the American film, *A Kiss Before Dying* – was wildly edgy by 1990s Bollywood standards. And

Shah Rukh Khan sunk his teeth into the roles of Ajay Sharma and Vicky Malhotra, alter-egos of the same person. The film started as – what seemed like – a frothy romance, but shocked audiences in a now-iconic scene where Shah Rukh Khan throws Shilpa Shetty off a roof. He then proceeds to romance her sister, Kajol, with his dimpled charm. A few more murders follow, to protect his alibi and identity. It is later revealed that he is hell-bent on taking revenge against the two women's father for ruining his family. While there was justification for his actions, *Baazigar* was different because Ajay/Vicky was a villain for a major part of the film. Even his revenge – killing an innocent daughter for her father's crimes – was way over the top. As over the top as the crazed energy SRK brought to the role, his calculated villainy giving way to an exceedingly violent climax that mutilated him. Probably for the first time in Hindi cinema, the 'hero' was reduced to a bloody mess.

If SRK's decision to take this role was surprising, the audience's reaction was even more so. The film was a runaway hit, and it was followed by *Darr* and *Anjaam* – both of which starred SRK in villainous roles. SRK used this 'villainous trilogy' to become a media sensation and the next superstar, before settling down into mushy and romantic roles. Hindi cinema experimented a lot more in the 2000s and 2010s, with major stars playing out-and-out negative roles. But all of that started with Shah Rukh Khan deciding to take on Ajay/Vicky – where no film hero was willing to go.

So, who were the stars who refused *Baazigar*? Akshay Kumar, for starters. The action star had starred in Abbas–Mustan's previous film, the very successful *Khiladi*, but was put off by the negative shades of this character. Anil Kapoor and Arbaaz Khan said no as well. The biggest star to say no to *Baazigar* was Salman Khan, whose father – screenwriter Salim Khan – suggested introducing the character's mother to justify his villainy. As it turned out, a mother was indeed added, but the makers didn't come back to Salman.

What would have been different if Salman Khan had played Ajay/Vicky? Salman himself answered this. 'There would be no Mannat standing on Bandstand today.'

Crime Master Gogo

Andaz Apna, 1994

Question: Who is Gogo's father?

Wait… What?

The story of *Andaz Apna Apna* started with producer Vinay Sinha wanting to make a film with the two teen heartthrobs of the day – Aamir Khan and Salman Khan – and director Rajkumar Santoshi wanting to direct something light after two tense thrillers (*Ghayal* and *Damini*). The resultant crazy caper didn't do too well initially, but over the years, it has become a cult classic with a loyal and ever-increasing fan-following. The film was a breathless mix of filmi tributes: *Amar Prem, Darr, Pyar Kiye Jaa, Sholay, Qayamat Se Qayamat Tak, Kalicharan* and – the funniest one – *Mr India*.

Mr India had become a huge hit (in 1987) and, when Rajkumar Santoshi started writing the script, Mogambo was a larger-than-life figure. And riffing on Mogambo's popularity, it was his *bhatija* who was the villain – Crime Master Gogo. The role was initially played by Tinnu Anand, but after shooting some portions, he had a problem with his dates and he had to be dropped from the film. Shakti Kapoor was brought in and he made the role his own. Wearing a cape and silly hairstyle, it was a role that embodied the relentlessly funny tone of the film. His signature line '*Khandani chor hoon, aaya hoon, kuch toh loot kar jaoonga*' became a catchphrase. His climactic fight with Salman Khan – in which they don't touch each other – was a masterclass in zaniness and comic timing. Gogo was one of four villains of *Andaz Apna Apna* – all with memorable quirks and idiosyncrasies. And yet, he stood out. It was a major departure for Shakti Kapoor, who usually played debauched louts and his was a last-minute entry into the cast. And he fit perfectly into the role. The film was in the making for nearly four years and, despite all the chaos of shoots and reshoots, Gogo remained unforgettable. And even now, when he does the '*Dhakki tiki dhakki tiki dhakki tiki dhaa*' dance in the climax, we fall off our chairs laughing. And indeed, that's how the cast also responded during the shoot. That scene had to be reshot several times because the lead players could not stop laughing.

Wait… You asked who Gogo's father was. What about that?

In Rajkumar Santoshi's initial draft, he had created a character called Zorambo, Mogambo's identical twin and exact opposite. While Mogambo was always happy and '*Mogambo khush hua*' was his punchline, Zorambo was never satisfied. Amrish Puri was approached to play this role too, in which he would wear white (to Mogambo's black) and have dark hair (to Mogambo's blonde). Zorambo was supposed to be the main villain of *Andaz Apna Apna* and Crime Master Gogo had a smaller part. But with both characters, the length of the film became a problem and eventually Zorambo had to be dropped. Zorambo's son – Mogambo *ka bhatija,* Crime Master Gogo – came to the fore.

Bulla

Gunda, 1998

In the mid-2000s, students of IIT Kharagpur took it upon themselves to take Gunda *to the top of IMDb ratings. Thousands of devotees of the cult of* Gunda *rated the film 10/10, and it was among the Top 3 films for a while (along with the likes of* The Godfather *and* The Shawshank Redemption*). As a tribute to their fandom, every sentence in this piece is taken (unchanged) from its reviews on IMDB.*

'If *Dr Strangelove* brought social satire into the mainstream, *Citizen Kane* pioneered political consciousness, *Rashomon* deconstructed the myth of authentic observation, *Dekalog* tweaked social mores, *One Flew Over the Cuckoo's Nest* overturned insanity on its head and *Kill Bill* celebrated the aesthetics of gut-spilling revenge, then there exists ONLY ONE Hindi movie that pays tribute to all these traditions without compromising on the inheritance of a typically Indian narration.'

'*Gunda* may simply appear to be a vendetta flick, where Bulla and his cronies rape or kill (sometimes both) Shankar's near and dear ones in the struggle to protect their rule over this dusty, broken town in India.'

'There are a whole gang of the villains, each with his unique style and dialogue delivery. Dialogues like "*Mera naam hai* Bullaaaa, *rakhta hoon* mail *khullaaaa*" are an extra point of the movie.'

'Mukesh Rishi, remembered for his role as Inspector Salim in *Sarfarosh*, proves why he is the coveted actor that he is.'

'Can anyone ever forget the scene where Bulla's sister dies and with her Bulla's tragic lament about choosing 300 chikna grooms for his sister?'

'Prabhuji is at his best (as ever), and the gang of villains outdo each other in terms of subtlety, but the real hero is the dialogue writer. The first 30 mins of the movie are full of pure gems in terms of poetry.'

'The dialogues are replete with similes, metaphors and rhyme, lending the movie a dialogic force. Viewing the movie thus becomes a lyrical journey.'

'The heart-wringing screams during the rapes, the dying requiems during murders, the brain-exploding twists, the transition through the landscapes in the parallel universe, the defying laws of gravity... I can go on showering laurels, but I will run out of adjectives.'

'The final fight is an amazing sequence, one that will put James Bond to shame. Mithunda, a coolie, arrives in a Maruti Esteem, while Bullaaa comes with 1000s of auto rickshaws.'

'With airport-to-shipyard teleport, half-hourly rape scenes, poetic exchanges, easily affordable bazookas, a brothel suspended in mid-air, and the mind warping auto-rickshaw blitzkrieg finale, *Gunda* is definitely a must watch. Every month.'

The Victoria House Inmate

Sarfarosh, 1999

A.C.P. Rathore raids Victoria House, suspected to be a clearing house for illegal arms. The main suspects escape, but some shopkeepers are arrested. Two of them seem to know about the criminal goings-on and are interrogated aggressively (read: beaten up black and blue). While shooting the scene, one of the actors – playing his first-ever role – asked if the camera could be kept away from his face. He wanted to do bigger roles soon and didn't want to be seen in a small part getting beaten up, that too half-naked.

Nawazuddin Siddiqui had come to Mumbai after graduating from National School of Drama, expecting to make it big, but the film world is ruthless and often oblivious to talent. Nawaz, unable to get any significant roles due to his 'non-hero' looks, started doing bit parts, and the role of the hapless Victoria House inmate was the first time he was seen on screen.

The second time was as a waiter – who is unable to figure out what 'that is all' means while taking the order – at a restaurant where Manoj Bajpayee and Raveena Tandon go to have dinner in *Shool*. He was with Manoj Bajpayee again in *Dil Pe Mat Le Yaar*, playing a garage mechanic and dancing in the background of a song. His TV 'debut' was as a murder suspect – who, yes, gets beaten up during interrogation – in a *CID* episode (called *The Case of Elusive Killer*). In *Munna Bhai MBBS*, he is a pickpocket who gets caught trying to filch Sunjay Dutt's wallet at the railway station and is beaten up by the crowd. Be it a goon in flashy shades in *Manorama Six Feet Under*, or a hero's friend (yes, he has done those too!) in *Family: Ties of Blood* and *Mudda: The Issue*, or a drunkard in *Ek Chalis Ki Last Local*, or a villager acting in Madhuri Dixit's play in *Aaja Nachle*... Nawazuddin acted in a variety of roles. His talent got an unusual showcase in the TV show *Star Bestsellers*, where he featured in an episode which was the first and only directorial venture of Irrfan Khan – someone he admired greatly and would soon share top billing with. By some estimates, he acted as bit players in about 30 films and TV shows before getting his major release in 2012, a long struggle even by the industry's cruel standards.

His partnership with Anurag Kashyap started with *Black Friday*, where he played Asgar Muqadam – Tiger Memon's secretary – who is, yet again, interrogated roughly by the police. *Dev.D* came next, where he is one half of the 'Patna ke Presleys' and sings the superhit '*Emosanal Attyachar*' song. Anurag Kashyap fell in love with his eyes and gave him a lead role in *Gangs of Wasseypur*. He shared equal billing with Manoj Bajpayee, with whom he had done his earliest bit parts. His first big release of 2012 – *Kahaani* – had him playing ACP Khan, a no-nonsense Intelligence Bureau officer not beyond doing a few tough interrogations himself!

By 2012, Nawaz was a star. Top directors were offering him meaty roles and films were planned around him. He ended the year playing a street-smart wastrel in *Talaash*, where Inspector Shekhawat (Aamir Khan) gets him into an interrogation room and gives him a tough time. Some things didn't change!

Nawazuddin Siddiqui in one of his many blink-and-miss roles, only in this one, you had to blink a little longer to miss him!

Image courtesy of Vinod Chopra Films

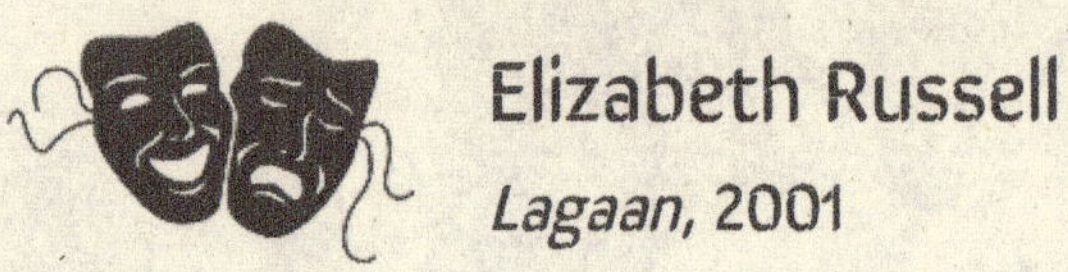

Elizabeth Russell

Lagaan, 2001

In May 2001, Britain's *The Guardian* published a 3,700-word diary of a 32-year-old British actress shooting for a Hindi film in India. Titled 'Love in a Hot Climate', the film was 'a period romantic comedy [sic] called *Lagaan*...the story of a dastardly British army captain who challenges the locals to a cricket match, the loser of which will pay the state's land tax – or *lagaan*.' Whether this piece evoked any major response in Britain is not known, but it created a furore in India because of the revelation that Aamir Khan's maiden production was a cricket story. We had seen the poster of a bunch of ragtag villagers staring defiantly at us. Now we suddenly noticed there were 11 of them.

Rachel Shelley auditioned for a part in a Hindi film, which her agent was very sceptical about. She was selected as the second lead, thus becoming only the second foreigner to land a lead in a major Bollywood production (after Kseniya Ryabinkina In *Mera Naam Joker*). She was part of a team of nearly 30 British actors who were selected to act in *Lagaan*. It was the highest-budget Bollywood film at that time, betting on a very unusual script by director Ashutosh Gowariker, which involved playing cricket in a period and rural setting.

The character of Elizabeth Russell, a British army captain's sister, who is sympathetic to the Indian cause, is unusual in every respect. For starters, she is part of a love triangle with Bhuvan (Aamir Khan) and Gauri (Gracey Singh), and her character is modelled on Radha, the consort of India's most famous love story. She also does a full-blown Bollywood dance number, though her part is in English (lyrics for which were written by Farhan and Zoya Akhtar) and performed like an opera.

The prep for *Lagaan* was intense – unlike Hindi films before that. Shelley (and several other British actors) had to learn Hindi to speak their lines for the film shot in synch-sound. While the production seemed highly prepped by Indian standards, Shelley complained bitterly about dialogue, costume and continuity issues during the gruelling shoot in Gujarat's Bhuj. She was even 'sanctimoniously reprimanded' by Aamir Khan for a meltdown she had on the sets. Despite last-minute changes in lines, she used cue boards to deliver them quite effectively. '*May toomsay pyar kurnay lugee hoo. Ha, Bhuvan, may toomsay pyar kurnay lugee hoo*' sounds odd only when written down!

Lagaan defied Shelley's agent's pessimism and went on to get nominated for an Oscar (for which Shelley was in LA). It also helped raise Indian cinema's profile internationally and sourcing international actors for Bollywood isn't an issue any more. In the last two decades, several foreigners have played substantial roles in Hindi films. Just as several foreigners have coached the Indian cricket team.

But Elizabeth Russell was the first!

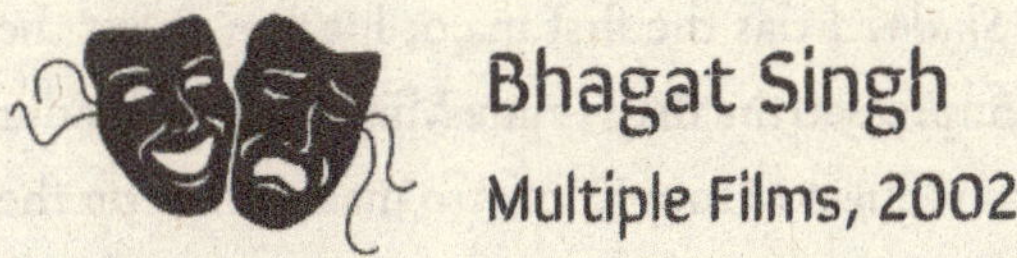

Bhagat Singh

Multiple Films, 2002

A 21-year-old killed a British police officer, exploded bombs at the Central Legislative Assembly while shouting patriotic slogans and then courted arrest to draw attention to their armed revolution. Jawaharlal Nehru said, 'He was like a spark that became a flame in a short time and spread from one end of the country to the other, dispelling the prevailing darkness everywhere.'

One of the first announcements of a film on Bhagat Singh was made by the legendary K. Asif in 1949. The film was supposed to be written by Khwaja Ahmad Abbas and it was billed as 'One man against the world's mightiest empire' in the announcements in trade magazines. It never got made. The first film on the revolutionary was *Shaheed-e-Azam Bhagat Singh* (1954) and Prem Abeed played the title role. Shammi Kapoor played the revolutionary in *Shaheed Bhagat Singh* (1963), but Manoj Kumar's *Shaheed* was the first major hit film about the martyr. The film impressed the then Prime Minister Lal Bahadur Shastri enough to request Manoj Kumar to make a film on the '*Jai jawan, jai kisaan*' slogan. In a way, it was Bhagat Singh who launched Manoj Kumar on his patriotic cinematic journey.

But what happened in 2002 was quite unprecedented – not only for Bhagat Singh but – for any potential subject of a biopic. Three films on the freedom fighter released within a week of one another. Sonu Sood played the title role of *Shaheed-e-Azam*, but it lacked star power and didn't get a major release. The other two films raced to their releases, which ended up being on the same day. Guddu Dhanoa's *23 March 1931: Shaheed* starred Bobby Deol. Rajkumar Santoshi's *The Legend of Bhagat Singh* started with Sunny Deol being considered for the title role, but it fell through due to disagreements over the fee. Eventually, Ajay Devgn played Bhagat Singh. After the success of several jingoistic films in the previous years, and a resurgence of nationalistic pride after Operation Vijay, the story of a dynamic revolutionary was a big draw. But two films releasing on the same day split the business and neither made substantial box-office collections.

Nevertheless, the films created a renewed interest in Bhagat Singh, despite charges of historical inaccuracies (including introducing a fiancée, something he steadfastly avoided in real life).

There was another film that featured him in an unconventional way. Rakeysh Omprakash Mehra's *Rang De Basanti* juxtaposed Bhagat Singh with modern-day youth and made us reconsider his actions in the context of present-day politics.

Four years after Bhagat Singh's hanging, it was observed by the British Intelligence Bureau that 'his photograph was on sale in every city and township and for a time rivalled in popularity with even that of Mr Gandhi himself'. Indeed, Bhagat Singh's hatted-moustachioed avatar is commonly seen in every street-side poster shop even today. If there was a flagging of interest in him, the films of 2002 brought him back not only into the pantheon of folk heroes, but political heroes as well. Bhagat Singh – the avowed Communist – is now the idol of every major political party from Left to Right.

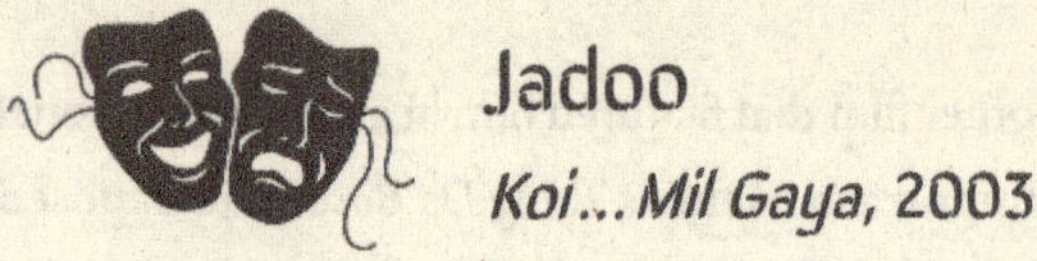

Jadoo

Koi... Mil Gaya, 2003

Indravadan Purohit, aka Chhote Ustad, aka Chhotu Dada, is an unfamiliar name, but a very familiar face for Hindi film fans. At 3'11", he is one of the shortest people in India (and was in the Limca Book of Records as one part of India's shortest couple). He had been in nearly 500 films, providing comic relief as a dwarf. In a film designed to resurrect the career of Hrithik Roshan, Purohit was called in to become an alien. He was flown to Australia for a screen test and had to undergo a strict diet regime to be able to fit inside the small alien suit that was being designed by an Australian special effects company. Sadly, he was not credited in the film.

After a sensational debut in *Kaho Naa... Pyaar Hai*, Hrithik Roshan's career had tanked with several high-profile flops. He then decided to get back with his father for their second film together. The story of a friendly alien – Jadoo – coming to Kasauli to help an intellectually disabled boy was different from the usual Hindi filmfare, but Rakesh Roshan packed enough Indian emotions into it to make it relatable to mainstream audiences. A scientist using 'Om' as the signal to connect with aliens, the alien ship signals causing an accident which affected the boy's mental faculties in the first place, and the alien helping the boy and his family as penance were as Indian as things got. And while Roshan Senior insisted that the film wasn't an 'Indian E.T.', the elements of a powerful but helpful alien, governmental agencies trying to capture it, and the shape and size of the alien itself were similar to the 'alien-meets-boy' template made famous by the Steven Spielberg film.

Rakesh Roshan didn't scrimp on the special effects and Jadoo is said to have cost 'as much as two other top heroes would have', estimates varying from Rs 2.5 crore to Rs 10 crores. James Colmer of Australia's Bimmini Special FX created the suit and spaceship of the alien, which would be partially controlled remotely and partially moved by Chhote Ustad from inside. The other special effects in the film were created at Bangalore's

Compudyne Winfosystems, under the supervision of Marc Kolbe and Craig Mumma – a team associated with films like *Independence Day* and *Godzilla.* The VFX had a strong Indian core, though. The spaceship – when viewed from the side – is the 'Om' symbol, which was also referenced in Jadoo's bracelet and necklace. The alien's nose–mouth design and large head subtly references Lord Ganesha (minus the trunk). And in an affectionate nod, Jadoo has an extra thumb – like Hrithik Roshan – which makes the boy feel he has a connection with him.

Koi... Mil Gaya became a superhero franchise and kickstarted 'sci-fi' as a genre in India, as well as the adoption of high-end visual effects in Bollywood. Sci-fi wasn't really a genre in Hindi cinema and, barring a few films in the 1960s (which explored space travel with very rudimentary visual effects), *Koi... Mil Gaya* could well be called the pioneering sci-fi Hindi film. In subsequent years, films like *Ra.One, Krrish, Krrish 3* and the Hindi-dubbed versions of Tamil films like *Robot* and *2.0* have really pushed the visual-effects envelope, if not the box-office one!

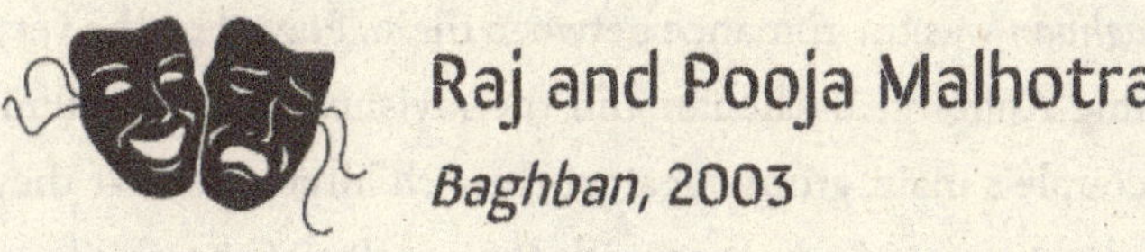

Raj and Pooja Malhotra

Baghban, 2003

From *Panchatantra* to modern-day advertising to WhatsApp forwards, an enduring concern in India is the abandonment of ageing parents. Parents who look after children, sacrificing their youth, are cruelly cast aside when the children become independent or get married to someone who doesn't understand the importance of taking care of your parents. A common plot was about doddering parents thrown out of homes – begging on the streets or making do with menial labour – till their children repent. Very famously, in the 1980s, the fading but still powerful superstar Rajesh Khanna played the title role of *Avtaar* where his sons threw him out of his home, and he rebuilt his fortune with the help of his wife and a loyal retainer.

Avtaar is one of many such films in the 1980s that explored this theme.

What differentiated all of them from Raj and Pooja Malhotra of *Baghban* was the romance between them. Played by the very dashing Amitabh Bachchan and the ravishing Hema Malini, the couple's main grouse against their children was that they were kept apart. And along with the cruelty of the children, Amitabh–Hema's romance was flamboyant and passionate – something that is hardly ever associated with older characters in Hindi cinema. Interestingly, the idea of the film was first conceived in the 1980s by B.R. Chopra, and the lead role was offered to Dilip Kumar (then a major star, looking to play older parts), but a suitable lead actress to cast opposite him couldn't be found. The early-2000s pairing of Amitabh and Hema was perfect. They sang two major hit songs, romanced each other on the telephone and did crazy things in love – almost reprising the romantic chemistry from their heydays. The film went on to become a big hit, but resonated even more with television and repeat audiences.

If it didn't start a trend of films about autumn romances, it at least created a space for romantic stories featuring older couples. Another hit couple from the yesteryears – Rishi Kapoor and Dimple Kapadia – starred in *Pyaar Mein Twist*, about an older couple facing resistance from their children regarding their romance. The makers of *Baghban* themselves made a 'sequel' – *Baabul* – in which an elderly couple tries matchmaking for their widowed daughter-in-law. In *Life in a Metro,* Dharmendra and Nafisa Ali played out a cute romantic story, never going out of sync with the overall modern, youthful nature of the film. If today we have Gajraj Rao and Neena Gupta playing a couple who are expecting a baby in their silver years (in *Badhaai Ho*), and the film becomes one of the biggest hits of the year, the seeds of that acceptance were sown by Raj and Pooja Malhotra in *Baghban.*

Maqbool

Maqbool, 2004

'*Gurujan, ho gaya,*' writer Abbas Tyrewala whispered excitedly when director Vishal Bhardwaj called him up from New Delhi railway station and told him about placing a Shakespearean play in the Mumbai underworld. For nearly two years before this, Bhardwaj, who was desperate to make a gangster film, read nearly every book, newspaper or magazine hoping to find a story. He found it when he was escorting his godson from Dehradun to Delhi and was stuck without anything to read. His godson offered a school book – *Tales from Shakespeare* by Charles and Mary Lamb – and Bhardwaj read the first Shakespeare story of his life: *Macbeth*.

William Shakespeare has appeared off and on in Hindi cinema, mostly through various permutations and combinations of *Romeo and Juliet*. A few exceptions – like Gulzar's *Angoor* reimagining *The Comedy of Errors* – aside, Shakespeare hadn't got as sumptuous a treatment as Bhardwaj's *Maqbool*. Be it transforming the three witches into two corrupt police officers or changing the character of Lady Macbeth from being Macbeth's wife to Duncan's mistress, the adapted screenplay was simultaneously faithful and creative. Bollywood, however, failed to see it. All major stars refused to play the role. But it was all in the stars because Bhardwaj later said, 'Thank god they did because only Irrfan Khan could be my *Maqbool*.'

Irrfan was selected only based on his performance in *Haasil* and he became the youngest NSD graduate in a cast full of them. Piyush Mishra, Pankaj Kapur, Om Puri and Naseeruddin Shah (who called the casting 'a masterstroke') put in splendid performances, and Irrfan held his own against all of them.

Maqbool was Irrfan's breakthrough performance in Indian cinema. While he had acted in the critically acclaimed international production, *The Warrior*, neither that nor any of his Indian films reached a critical mass of noticeability. Despite a lukewarm box-office response, *Maqbool* was breathlessly reviewed by critics all over, and kicked off a renewed interest in

Shakespeare ... and Irrfan. Bhardwaj himself completed a trilogy of films based on Shakespeare, all receiving rave reviews with several other film-makers also going back to the Bard. After *Maqbool*, Irrfan's parts became meatier, his projects became bigger and it was the beginning of his journey in becoming India's most effortless genius in acting. Bhardwaj and Irrfan reunited with *Haider*, based on *Hamlet*, in which Irrfan played Roohdar – an eerie representation of the Ghost.

Maqbool reached a cult status and a large part of it is due to Irrfan's performance as the guilt-ridden, tragic hero, who spoke more with his eyes than with his voice. How good was the performance, really? Watching Irrfan perform, Naseeruddin Shah – accepted as one of India's greatest actors – used to think of himself as Antonio Salieri and Irrfan as Mozart. Yes, that good!

Mohandas Karamchand Gandhi

Lage Raho Munna Bhai, 2006

A freedom fighter goes into coma after being hit on the head by a policeman. He wakes up 50 years later in a hospital and asks, 'How is Bapu? Has he ended his fast?'

This was the idea Rajkumar Hirani had for the script of a satire set in present-day India seen through the eyes of a Gandhian. With the smashing success of the first Munna Bhai film, this idea evolved into the Gandhian meeting Munna and Circuit. And finally, the Gandhian became Gandhi himself!

The 1980s Indian kid's acquaintance with Gandhi has primarily been through Richard Attenborough's classic, dubbed in Hindi and religiously shown every 2nd October on Doordarshan. With the advent of private television channels, this annual ritual waned, and Gandhi largely became the guy on our currency notes. He was – as Circuit memorably deadpanned – just a guy born on a dry day.

Director Raju Hirani and his co-writer, Abhijat Joshi, took this kind-of-forgotten, nearly irrelevant hero of our freedom struggle and recreated a wonderfully modern, humorous Father of the Nation who appears in 21st century India – visible only to a Mumbai goon – and solves daily problems with his unique mixture of truthfulness and courage. They even coined a phrase for it: *Gandhigiri*!

Getting an actor (Marathi legend Dilip Prabhavalkar) to look the part with training and make-up was easy. Getting Gandhi to devise solutions for corrupt government departments, get-rich-quick schemes, shady property deals and modern love was tricky, but they managed to do that too ... with ideas that were actually Gandhi's! As part of the preparation, Joshi read pretty much all the major works of Gandhi, including a 23-volume diary of his secretary. Then came the task of framing Gandhi's solutions in the trademark Mumbai *tapori* lingo – made famous by Munna and Circuit – and once that was done, *Gandhigiri* became a thing!

The concept of 'turning the other cheek' was translated into the act of giving roses and get-well-soon cards to the corrupt, those with poor manners, and the lazy and cowardly. This, in fact, became a popular act of resistance for many in India. Regional Transport Offices across the country – known for their corrupt practices in issuing driving licenses – received roses from helpless applicants trying to shame officials into doing their duty. Electricity Departments, Public Works Departments and even private sector service providers received roses and cards from their customers. The phenomenon went global when Indians in the USA sent roses to the immigration office, where their green-card applications were held up. Police departments started handing roses to traffic violators, hoping to reform them in the long run. And, in the long run – 14 years after the film – students protesting against the CAA–NRC handed roses to Delhi Police officials, after the force was accused of brutally beating up protestors.

We haven't yet taken Gandhi's teachings to heart. *Gandhigiri* will have to be around for a while.

Dilip Prabhavalkar as Bapu. Gandhi has a larger-than-life presence in modern India, even in tapori Munna's India.

Image courtesy of Vinod Chopra Films

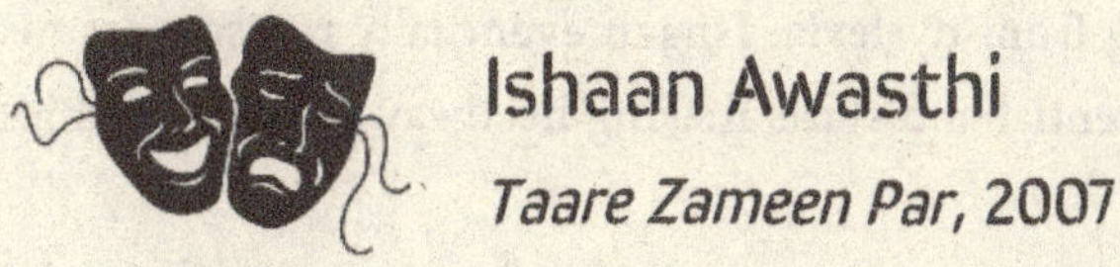

Ishaan Awasthi

Taare Zameen Par, 2007

After *Taare Zameen Par* released, Amole Gupte – creative director of the film – received a call from a rickshaw-puller from Lucknow. The man cried on the phone and, in between sobs, he explained how he had been perceiving his son wrong all this while. The film's message about how children silently suffer from dyslexia opened his eyes to his son's disadvantage and his insensitivity to it. *Taare Zameen Par* was one hell of an eye-opener!

Ishaan Awasthi is the younger son of a conventional middle-class family obsessed with studying hard and doing well. Ishaan's obvious skills at art are overlooked as his poor spelling and bad handwriting make him a 'difficult' child both at home and school. He is sent off to a boarding school, where his situation worsens, till a compassionate teacher arrives and understands that Ishaan is suffering from dyslexia. Ishaan eventually rediscovers his artistic potential and starts making headway in his academics as well.

It is a great testament to the makers' courage that the entire first half of the film depended on Ishaan's suffering, and one of India's biggest stars, Aamir Khan – playing the teacher – appeared only in the second half. In a way, this was box-office suicide, but with an acting performance like Darsheel Safary's, it made utter sense.

Darsheel Safary had seen the advertisement for the film's audition in his dance class at Shiamak Davar's academy. Amole Gupte had already met and befriended him, making his selection almost a formality. The casting was a stroke of genius, with Safary – his unruly mop of hair, wild eyes and buckteeth – not meeting the conventional standards of filmi cuteness. But Ishaan's strength – his art – was built almost like a superpower. An acclaimed artist, Samir Mondal, was brought in to help create Ishaan's paintings. His art was a stunning mix of creativity and technique that almost ached to come out and be seen – not only by Ishaan, but the audience as well.

The tragedy of Ishaan was – unlike so many characters – his disability was invisible. Unlike Hindi cinema's previous attempts to raise awareness about disabilities – Mehmood's *Kunwara Baap* about polio, Sunil Dutt's *Dard Ka Rishta* about cancer and Revathy's *Phir Milenge* about AIDS – *Taare Zameen Par* reached a massive audience thanks to Aamir's star power and was one of the top grossers of the year. The impact of the film was such that schools, state education boards and even the Ministry of Women & Child Development made it mandatory for teachers to watch the film. *Taare Zameen Par* went beyond identifying a disability like dyslexia and removing the stigma associated with it. Many schools serving different social strata, in urban and rural centres, reconsidered the way they assessed their students and learnt to deal with children with special abilities. And how to discover the stars in their eyes!

All this triggered by a nine-year-old boy who made you cry when he cried. And made your day when he laughed – his eyes and teeth gleaming!

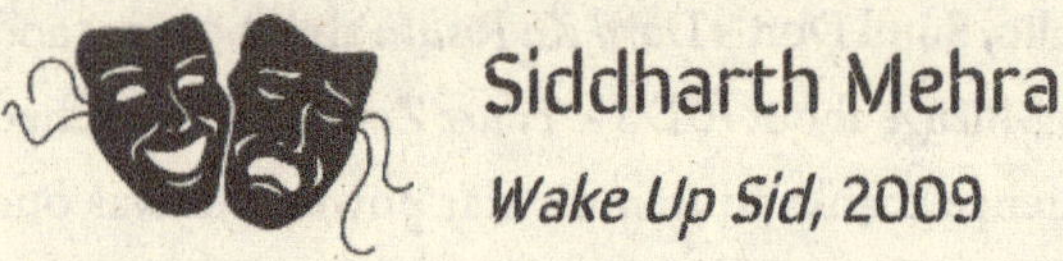

Siddharth Mehra

Wake Up Sid, 2009

Ayan Mukerji and Ranbir Kapoor grew up in adjacent buildings in Mumbai's Pali Hill, even though they didn't know each other then. They were the same age, both from illustrious film families and had shades of the entitled man-child that Ayan's first script was about. Within minutes of finishing the script narration, Ranbir had agreed to do the film and had 'become' Sid by the time the first photo shoot happened. Ayan created playlists for him, gifted him DVDs and comic books that would be liked by Sid – all of which Ranbir just 'got'. The actor himself suggested the title *Wake Up Sid,* which was perfect for the film – much better than *Badmaash* that Ayan had come up with.

Ranbir Kapoor was selected for his 'easy, naughty, dream-like quality' that Ayan envisaged for his hero. 'Hero' is probably a misnomer for the character, which was the exact antithesis of the filmi hero that we grew up with. After years of an exultant hero shouting 'Maa, *main* pass *ho gaya*', Sid flunks his B.Com. final exams and isn't even able to say it loud in the film. 'Maa, *mere* results *aa gaye*' is the cryptic line with which Sid shatters the heroic image of the filmi hero. After years of the poor hero joining the first job he lands in order to take care of his family, Sid walks out of his father's flourishing bathroom-fittings business. 'The place just wasn't me,' he shrugs to his friend. Sid wears a Beavis and Butt-Head t-shirt on his first day at work – part of his childish, pop-culture binging persona. And with this, Ranbir Kapoor created a modern counterpoint to his own father's wardrobe of sweaters for romantic films.

If *Dil Chahta Hai* made rich people cool in Hindi cinema, *Wake Up Sid* was the beacon for so-called underachievers, who find their passion beyond living up to society's expectations. Sid finds his perfect foil in 'a new girl in the city' Aisha Banerjee (Konkona Sen Sharma), who arrives from Calcutta with a clear ambition and a clearer plan on how to get there. Sid is dreamy, while Aisha is practical. Sid is the kid, while Aisha is the older woman. She gets him a job, teaches him to take care of himself and inspires him to start cooking eggs. By the end of the film, Sid has stopped ordering pizza and started cooking pasta at home instead. Also, he has graduated from Marvel comics to Murakami.

Wake Up Sid is based on Ayan Mukerji's own nostalgia for his college life. It doesn't have – as Ayan himself says – 'the narrative drama commercial Hindi cinema demands'. In fact, it is just a collection of experiences with a very thin storyline that is almost like an anti-film. In a filmi *duniya* used to bombastic tributes to Bombay, it creates an understated ode to Mumbai. In a filmworld obsessed with heroes finding the meaning of life itself, it gives us a hero who simply finds himself.

Bhairav Singh

Udaan, 2010

Unable to make it big in cinema, Ronit Roy had moved to television and had become one of the busiest stars of daily soaps. His neighbour, Anurag Kashyap, casually offered him a small role in a film he was producing. Roy read the script, liked it and didn't think too much about it. He had come back from a shoot one night at 2 a.m., but was woken by his wife at 6 a.m. because Kashyap had come to meet him. Scratching his beard in his usual fidgety fashion, Kashyap told Roy that he was going to meet UTV and he would be playing the cruel father's – instead of the uncle's, as initially discussed – role. And just like that, Hindi television's busiest actor went off to a small town in Jharkhand to shoot for 39 days.

From the moment we see Bhairav Singh standing on a railway overbridge at the station, the first word that comes to mind is 'imposing'. He runs a small factory in the industrial town of Jamshedpur, is emotionally cut-off from his family and tries to physically abuse them into submission. He remarries – twice – trying to find love, trying to run the world and its people the way he wants to.

Director Vikramaditya Motwane said that Roy's real achievement lay in 'taking a villainous character but giving [him] a sense of pathos'. Bhairav Singh is a despicable man for the entire film, with very little to redeem him. But we cannot help but feel a bit sorry for him. Ronit Roy returned the director's compliment by noting that 90 per cent of the performance came from the script. It is indeed an exceptionally written character, where hints of the genesis of his brutal behaviour come out in snippets throughout the film. There are hints of a cycle of violence, where his father also physically disciplined him into submission and he uses that as justification. In a brilliantly written scene, Bhairav tells his son he came to visit him at the boarding school, but couldn't find anything to say. He didn't want to interrupt his happiness, Bhairav says – making his sadness and helplessness come across beautifully.

The preparation and shooting were intense. Roy, being a television actor, was used to clear dialogue delivery. Motwane nudged him out of his comfort zone and raised his hackles by quietly asking Rajat Barmecha (playing Rohan, Bhairav's son) to interrupt his dialogues. Motwane insisted that Barmecha and Roy didn't socialize with each other during the shoot, so that their animosity gets built.

Barmecha said that Roy was so deep into the character for whom violence was so casual that he would slap him out of turn, without the script demanding it. And, in a climactic fight, where Bhairav is punched by his son, Barmecha broke Roy's nose – it even required surgery later.

Udaan is a remarkable film and Bhairav Singh is a remarkable character. Hindi cinema has always had authoritarian fathers, but none were as realistically brutal as this one. The real horror of Bhairav Singh comes across when we see Rohan bullying his younger stepbrother in the early scenes and wonder if he will become another Bhairav. But the triumph of *Udaan* is when he chooses to take a different path. And takes flight.

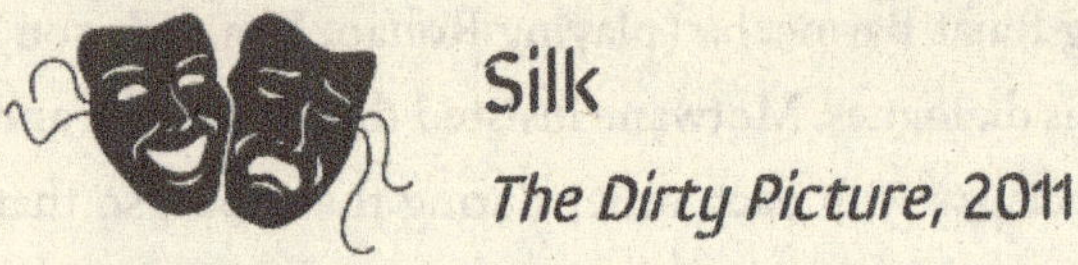

Silk

The Dirty Picture, 2011

About Southern siren Silk Smitha's mass appeal, film historian Randor Guy said, 'Films that had lain in cans for years were sold by the simple addition of a Silk Smitha song.'

This is exactly the beginning of Silk's rise to stardom in Milan Luthria's *The Dirty Picture.* Vidya Balan plays Reshma, an aspirant in the Tamil film industry, who performs so raunchily as a backup dancer that her song – added later – rescues the fortunes of what is initially a flop film. While it wasn't officially called a Silk Smitha biopic, it was released – as a tribute – on her birthday, 2nd December.

Writer Rajat Aroraa said, 'It is a biopic in as much as when you write about doctors, you would want to include a famous surgery that actually happened as a hub around which fictionalized events turn.'

What started as a screenplay about the soft-porn industry of the 1980s became a 'women-oriented perspective of the film industry' of the times. Director Milan Luthria, fresh off the success of *Once Upon a Time in Mumbai,* was roped in for his ability to create a period ambience.

The lead role was offered to Bipasha Basu and Kangana Ranaut, before coming to Vidya Balan – who shared great personal rapport with producer Ekta Kapoor (thanks to Vidya getting launched in an Ekta Kapoor serial). She was an unlikely choice for the role of a sex symbol because most of her previous roles were conventional, even conservative. Her first outing on the edge was in *Ishqiya,* in which she played a foul-mouthed scheming seductress, but nothing came close to the buxom belle of *The Dirty Picture.*

A young girl runs away from a conservative home and enters the movies. She cultivates a sexy image, and willingly succumbs to the casting coach to become the industry's biggest crowd-puller. Her success in films doesn't lead to a happy personal life. She craves for love as well as respect, till she ends her life in a fit of depression. This was also the life story of Silk Smitha, who died by suicide, unable to stay on in an industry which constantly put her down. This tragic story was retold in more positive terms, showing the film's Silk as a woman who gave it back as good as she got. Vidya Balan's performance won awards left, right and centre, and Rajat Aroraa's lines were the talk of the town. And, in an industry fixated on male stars, it was one of the top grossers of the year and established Vidya Balan as one of the few female stars who could pull an entire film on her own.

Also, in an industry fixated on size zero, Vidya Balan did something subversive by putting on 12 kilos for the role. While Hindi film heroines of yore always looked well-fed and well-endowed, a bulging mid-riff and pronounced love handles were always frowned upon. In *The Dirty Picture*, Silk had all that and more. Balan herself exuded a killer attitude that seemed to match the character she was playing. An interviewer asked about her performance: 'You faked an orgasm not once but twice? What were you thinking of?'. Vidya Balan saucily replied, 'Let's just say it had been a while since I had met my boyfriend, Siddharth [Roy Kapur].'

Ooh la la!

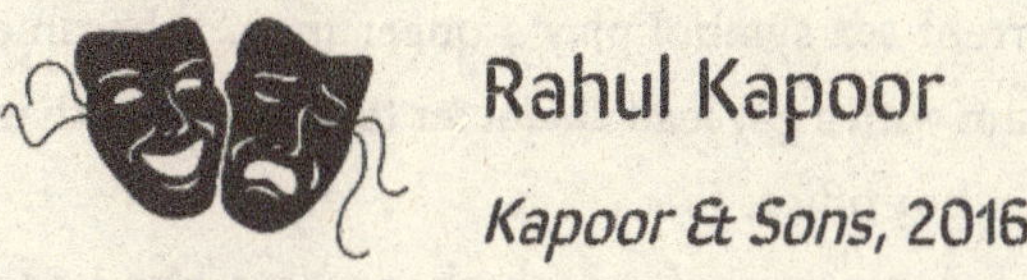

Rahul Kapoor

Kapoor & Sons, 2016

Fawad Khan's popularity in India started soaring with the availability of his television series, *Zindagi Gulzar Hai*, on a newly launched channel called Zindagi that was meant exclusively for international shows. Pakistani shows topped the popularity charts and Fawad Khan – playing the handsome Zaroun Junaid – became a sensation in India. His Hindi debut followed soon after (Shashanka Ghosh's *Khoobsurat*), but no one has really made it in Bollywood unless one has been offered a Dharma Productions film. And Fawad Khan was signed for two.

In March 2016, Shashi Tharoor introduced a private member bill (for the second time in three months) to decriminalize homosexuality. It was unceremoniously voted out even as the debate against the colonial-era Article 377 heated up. Exactly a week later, *Kapoor & Sons* released, and became a major milestone in the depiction of homosexuality in Hindi cinema. By having a current sex symbol play a queer man, it became the first Hindi film with a gay lead character to gross more than ₹100 crore at the box office.

Bollywood's depiction of queer characters has been problematic to say the least. It started with an obscure film called *Badnam Basti* (1971), but it was neither directed well nor promoted – and disappeared into oblivion. Films made on homosexuality – *Fire, My Brother... Nikhil, I Am, Aligarh* – were art house in appeal. Karan Johar's own productions – *Kal Ho Naa Ho, Dostana* – did their bit to trivialize homosexuality by poking fun at it, which was a standard component of Bollywood humour for ages. In *Student of the Year*, Rishi Kapoor became the first mainstream 'hero' to play a queer character, though it was exaggerated to the point of being a caricature.

Shakun Batra's *Kapoor & Sons* (co-written with Ayesha DeVitre) stood out because the queer character's issues were not key to the film. It was one of the interesting sub-plots in an intricate tapestry, and the film was hailed by critics and audiences for its a crackling ensemble cast playing a dysfunctional family – everyone with their own set of problems. Fawad Khan's Rahul

– the elder son – was his mother's 'perfect *bachcha*', a successful author and everyone's favourite. In a masterful script, his visage slowly unravels as a murky incident from the past comes to light and his mother accidentally stumbles upon his sexuality. The sexuality itself is a spoiler because the character betrays none of the so-called tell-tale signs that Bollywood saddles its queer characters with. It is only with hindsight that we realize the character was trying to come out to his family and failing.

And the coming out itself is a goosebumps-inducing scene. As his mother (Ratna Pathak Shah) tries to get her mind around her perfect *bachcha's* 'blemishes', Rahul asks her the most defining question of all coming-outs: '*Aap ko mere jhoot se gham hai ya mere asliyat se?*'

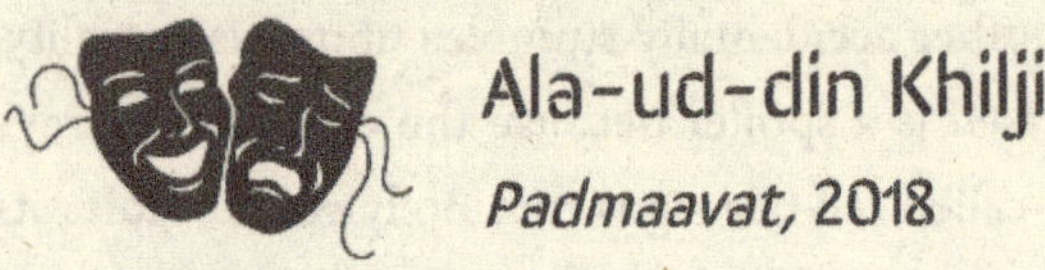

Ala-ud-din Khilji

Padmaavat, 2018

'Don't you want to play a character who has 75-kilo balls?' was Sanjay Leela Bhansali's clinching pitch. He was trying to convince Ranveer Singh into playing Ala-ud-din Khilji, the incorrigible villain of *Padmaavat.* Ranveer Singh was in a happy space in his personal life, and had just come off a light role in *Befikre.* He didn't want to get into a dark zone. He also had the usual apprehensions of playing a villain and what it would do to his career. But Bhansali finally got his Khilji.

Based on Malik Muhammad Jayasi's epic poem, *Padmaavat* is a story of futile Rajput valour in the face of a Muslim onslaught. The story itself is fictional, and Rani Padmavati never existed in all probability. But the story of love, passion and obsession was very attractive to Bhansali. He worked on it for several years, searching for the ideal cast.

Bhansali's Ala-ud-din Khilji was a full-on filmi villain, though – as he explained to Ranveer – a sexy one. *Padmaavat*'s Khilji was a crazed lover. A hedonistic gourmand. A barbaric warrior. A flamboyant dancer. And almost a petulant teenager. *Padmaavat* reduced the complex history of a Delhi Sultan and his Rajasthan campaign to a simplistic tale of love and honour, for which it received a lot of flak from historians. Khilji repelling the Mongol invasions got reduced to one stormy war. His infatuation with Malik Kafur, who became his commander and vizier, became a series of titillating sequences. When the Khilji of Shyam Benegal's *Bharat Ek Khoj* heard about a beautiful Rajput princess, he said that the maids of his 1,600 wives were probably more beautiful. This Khilji, on the other hand, coveted Padmavati by hearing stories of her beauty and laid a six-month-long siege to win her. And finally killed her husband in a dishonourable duel. Only to realize she has committed *jauhar* (ritual mass suicide) to avoid capture.

Ranveer's prep to play this simplistic reduction of a complex character was something else, though. He spent 21 days in isolation. He read up on lives of tyrants and about genocides to replicate the psychology of the ruthless commander of a marauding army. During this period, he also decided to have the physique of a silverback gorilla. For this, he bulked up by following – what he called – the 'Khilji workout': 'eat red meat and lift weights'. The obsessive prep and the 45 days of shooting (usually in bulky costumes and heavy make-up) had turned his mind into mush. So much so that he had to take psychiatric help.

Despite filmi concessions, it was very courageous of Ranveer Singh to play a villain with homosexual undertones. Especially in Bollywood, where hero and villain are two airtight clusters. Add to that a controversial production, with imminent danger of getting attacked by mobs and the film getting taken off theatres. Maybe Ranveer Singh does have 75-kilo balls, after all!

Ranveer Singh as Sultan. A top star playing a demented, deviant despot – a character as enigmatic as it was fictional.

Image copyright: Viacom 18 Studios

Bibliography

Ahmed, Rauf. *Shammi Kapoor: The Game Changer*. Noida: Om Books International, 2016.

Bhardwaj, Vishal, and Abbas Tyrewala. *Maqbool: The Original Screenplay*. Noida: Harper Collins Publishers India, 2014.

Bhatia, Sidharth. *Amar Akbar Anthony: Masala, Madness and Manmohan Desai*. Harper Collins Publishers India.

Bhattacharjee, Anirudha, and Balaji Vittal. *R.D. Burman: The Man, the Music*. Noida: Harper Collins Publishers India, 2011.

Bhattacharya, Rinki Roy. *Bimal Roy: The Man Who Spoke in Pictures*. New Delhi: Penguin.

Bose, Mihir. *Bollywood: A History*.

Chatterjee, Gayatri. *Mother India*. British Film Institute.

Chopra, Vidhu Vinod, and Abhijat Joshi. *Unscripted: Conversations on Life and Cinema*. Gurgaon: Penguin Random House, 2021.

Dwyer, Rachel. *Yash Chopra: Fifty Years in Indian Cinema*. New Delhi: Roli Books, 2002.

Garga, Bhagwan Das. *So Many Cinemas: The Motion Picture in India.* Mumbai: Eminence Designs, 1996.

Jain, Madhu. *The Kapoors: The First Family of Indian Cinema.* New Delhi: Penguin, 2009.

Manwani, Akshay. *Music, Masti, Modernity: The Cinema of Nasir Husain.* Noida: Harper Collins Publishers India, 2016.

Paranjpye, Sai. *A Patchwork Quilt: A Collage of My Creative Life.* Noida: Harper Collins Publishers India, 2020.

Roychoudhury, Amborish. *In a Cult of Their Own: Bollywood beyond Box Office.* New Delhi: Rupa, 2018.

Singh, Jai Arjun. *Jaane Bhi Do Yaaro: Seriously Funny since 1983.* Noida: Harper Collins Publishers India, 2013.

Singh, Jai Arjun. *The World of Hrishikesh Mukherjee: The Filmmaker Everyone Loves.* Gurgaon: Penguin, 2016.

Upadhyay, Karishma. *Parveen Babi: A Life.* Gurgaon: Hachette India, 2020.

Vinod Chopra Films. *Lage Raho Munna Bhai: The Original Screenplay.* New Delhi: Om Books International, 2010.

Wenner, Dorothee. *Fearless Nadia: The True Story of Bollywood's Original Stunt Queen.* New Delhi: Penguin, 2005.

Zankar, Anil. *Mughal-e-Azam: Legend as Epic.* Noida: Harper Collins Publishers India, 2013.

Acknowledgements

Abhishek Dubey, Ajit Andhare and Akhil Jain for their help with sourcing the images.

Thomas Abraham, Poulomi Chatterjee, Swarnima Narayan and Ansila Thomas of Hachette India, for indulging me at every turn and turning my ramblings into a dream series.

Echo Chamber, Sobuj Sangho, Kwiz Group, for fuelling many trivial pursuits.

Rita Chaudhuri, Shivaramakrishnan K and Nilendu Misra, for always being ready to talk movies.

Trishna, Dyujoy and Drishti Chaudhuri, for always being there.